EARLY RAILWAYS OF SCOTLAND

ANTHONY DAWSON AND ED BETHUNE

AMBERLEY

Cover: Artwork by Peter Savee.

First published 2025

Amberley Publishing
The Hill, Stroud,
Gloucestershire, GL5 4EP

www.amberley-books.com

ISBN: 978 1 3981 2319 9 (print)
ISBN: 978 1 3981 2320 5 (ebook)

British Library Cataloguing in Publication Data.
A catalogue record for this book is available from the British Library.

Typeset in 10pt on 13pt Celeste.
Typesetting by SJmagic DESIGN SERVICES, India.
Printed in the UK.

Appointed GPSR EU Representative:
Easy Access System Europe Oü, 16879218
Address: Mustamäe tee 50, 10621, Tallinn, Estonia
Contact Details: gpsr.requests@easproject.com,
+358 40 500 3575

Contents

Foreword

On a rail journey from York to Edinburgh in around 1974, my parents kept my brother and I entertained by getting us to look out for interesting features along the route. At Darlington we noted the two Stockton & Darlington Railway locomotives *Locomotion* and *Derwent,* which appeared to represent the first railway dating to 1825.

However, later in the journey we passed the site of the 1745 Battle of Prestonpans. Here my father – a railwayman with a keen interest in railway history – told us about a railway which had played a part in that battle. But how could a railway have been involved in a battle eighty years before the opening of the first railway?

It soon became evident that railways were much older than I had imagined. Scotland clearly had an important early railway story. Indeed, the railway that played a part in that battle, the Tranent–Cockenzie Waggonway, was Scotland's first railway, and had opened in 1722, over a century before the Stockton & Darlington.

The growth of railways across Scotland in the late eighteenth century was impressive. In 1811, the Kilmarnock & Troon Railway carried its first passengers and five years later commissioned the first steam locomotive to run in Scotland. By the turn of the twentieth century, Glasgow was making more locomotives than any other place in Europe.

In the story of early railways, Scotland matters. That story needs to be told. Ed Bethune and Anthony Dawson do just that in this excellent book. They reveal the early development of Scotland's railway using the latest research – archaeological and archival – in an engaging, concise and informative way and show how the country played a key role in the growth of a railway network that changed the world.

Andrew McLean
National Railway Museum

Chapter 1

Origins

Tulloch and the Inveresk Question

Before getting to railways which we know were built, it is helpful to spend some time on the ones which were not, or rather, that we have no evidence for having been built. The records which can give us information about such early railways are typically scant, however, there are some which can tell us a little about some projects which seemingly

Cockenzie Harbour, *c.* 1870, unknown artist. The salt pan building is in use with smoke from the chimney and steam permeating the roof, while coal waggons and a coal drop gantry are visible on the quayside. (Reproduced with permission of East Lothian Council Museums Service)

never came to fruition. The first railways in England were introduced during the 1560s by German-speaking immigrants at silver mines in the Lake District. These were guide-pin railways, but the first railed-ways were likely developed at Broseley in Shropshire around 1600 and later at Wollaton in Nottinghamshire around 1604, later spreading to the north-east of England by 1610. The first railway in Wales was about the same time, thus Thomas Tulloch's new 'ingyne' of 1606 would fit perfectly with this timeline.

To understand the context in which the development of early railways in Scotland came about, we need to look at the early coal industry which had been established around the monastic communities of the Lothians. Of particular interest, on account of what was to come later, in around 1200, the monks at Newbattle Abbey were granted by Earl Seyer de Quincy the right to mine coal and make salt in the lands of Prestongrange. Specifically, the lands are described accordingly:

> As the burn of Whytrig falls into the sea, on the east, to the marches of the Abbot of Dunfermline's lands of Inveresch (Inveresk) and Ponttekyn (Pinkie), namely, as the rivulet runs from Fauside to the sea, and as I, in presence of good men, perambulated the march between my own mains and Meduflat, and cast ditches for a memorial.

This 'rivulet', or stream, running from the Fa'side area to the east, reaches the coast at Seton and sets the geographical context of the early coal and salt industries in the area. This is quite a large tract of land and would later become the industrial portion of the Winton Estate.

However, in 1606, another intriguing reference from the Privy Council of Scotland grants, or instructs, a man named Thomas Tulloch permission to explore a new technology which could transform the transportation of coal in the very same area: 'imployit the maist pairt of his youth in uncuth nations in searching and learning the knawledge for making and practizeing of ingynis and workis for the commodious and aisle transporting of coillis betix the colpotis, sey and salt panes of this realm'. Also, that it was 'ane work and ingyne nocht known in this kingdom at na time of before'.

The implication of this intriguing statement is that Tulloch should spend time in 'uncouth nations', possibly abroad or south of the border, gaining the knowledge to be able to construct the 'engines and works' to be able to transport coal from the 'coalpits' to the 'sea and the salt pans'.

This fascinating turn of events describes a formalised attempt to improve the transit of coal to the most important early-modern industry, saltmaking, for which it was the fuel required for the insatiable furnaces which boiled the brine. It describes a waggonway, of which there were none in the nation of Scotland at the time. It seems likely that news of waggonways abroad or the one at Wollaton Hall, Nottinghamshire, constructed just two years earlier, had reached Scotland, and that it was the intention of a national body to build one in the area of Inveresk.

However, this is the only information relating to the possibility of a waggonway being built at this time; there is no record of actual construction; no record of completion; nothing to indicate operation of a railway; and, crucially, no cartographical evidence to suggest this line ever existed.

So, it seems highly unlikely that Tulloch's research into this wonder-technology ever came to fruition. However, the seed had been sown, and it would not be long before this part of Scotland would become the birthplace of the nation's railways.

Salt

As already mentioned, in early-modern Scotland, production of sea salt was the single largest industry in the country. This was a commodity essential primarily for food preservation, but also for industrial and scientific uses such as pottery, glassmaking and medicine.

Easily accessible coal, close to the sea, provided the ideal environment for the development of salt works. Blazing fires under pans of boiling brine were a common sight, especially around the Firth of Forth. A few towns to this day, such as Prestonpans and Saltcoats, still bear the place names which give an indication to their industrial past.

Around the year 1630, George, the 3rd Earl of Winton, built a substantial salt works consisting of at least twelve salt pans at Cockenzie 'where ane had never been before'. However, the long saltmaking history of this coastline being beyond doubt, the earl was not taking a plunge into the unknown. This had been a salt-producing area for centuries and the precedence and skill set was already present. The salt works operated with some degree of success and was passed on through the family for generations.

In 1707 the political union between Scotland and England was enacted. As a commodity vital to the economy, salt became a hotly debated issue. The last session of the Scottish Parliament was used to discuss the English salt tax that would be imposed on Scotland following the union. It was hoped this would derail plans for the union. Jacobite sympathisers chanted the slogan 'No union, no malt tax, no salt tax' in an effort to drum up support.

A Salt Duty bill was passed by the newly formed British Parliament in 1713, and heavy taxes were imposed on Scottish salt, quickly leading to salt smuggling to avoid paying the expensive price. Numerous gaugers, or salt excisemen, were employed to oversee the trade at the salt works and to prevent salt going missing.

A cutaway model of a typical salt pan house.

Saltmaking Process

The making of sea salt crystals by boiling brine is a laborious and intensive industrial process which requires a phenomenal amount of fuel. Seawater is collected in rock-cut ponds on the shoreline called 'bucket pots', before being bucketed into cisterns on wooden platforms immediately on the landward side. From there it runs through a sluice-controlled wooden channel called a 'spout' into the salt pan house, within which there is an iron pan sitting atop a furnace area.

The iron pans were huge, being a maximum size of about 18 ft x 9 ft, with the furnace and flue systems beneath for heat distribution covering a similar area. A furnace this size requires a great deal of fuel, particularly with salt being made virtually twenty-four hours a day, seven days a week (with the exception of Sundays). With each tonne of salt produced reputedly requiring around 4 tonnes of fuel, the demand for the coal from the nearby pits was high.

By 1716, the salt works at Cockenzie had become the largest in Scotland, producing around 10 per cent of the country's salt: 20,000 bushels (500 tonnes) per year, with 2,000 tonnes of coal being burned in the furnaces. All this coal was transported to the salt pans from local mines by horse and cart or packhorse.

The custodianship of the Wintons came to an end when George, the 5th Earl, forfeited his inherited estates including the salt works, after supporting the 1715 Jacobite rising. The forfeited Scottish estates were auctioned off, and this accordingly provided an opportunity for a new owner to acquire the industries.

The 'Auld Kirk' Salt Pan House at Cockenzie during excavations in 2021. Note the twin ash pits which were part of the brander furnaces. (Sally Pentecost)

A modern one-third-scale salt pan at Cockenzie, operated using eighteenth-century methods by the 1722 Waggonway Project.

The York Buildings Company of London

The York Buildings Company was an English business based at York Buildings, near Westminster. It was established in 1695 primarily to supply London households with water pumped from the Thames. In 1719, following a careful audit of the Scottish estates conducted by company agents, the company raised money from investors to purchase several of the land packages forfeited after the 1715 Jacobite rising. The estate at Winton commanded the not insignificant sum of £50,482. Having invested so heavily, investors were keen to see a quick return, and having already identified the potential of the industries here, a modernisation and improvement plan was put in place.

This development saw the introduction of a wooden waggonway. This would be Scotland's first railway to come to fruition despite the previous, and much earlier, plans for the like of Inveresk, just a few miles away on the same stretch of coastline.

The aim was to increase the efficiency of coal transit from the pits at Tranent Muir to the salt works on the coast, with the additional benefit of a well-established harbour and shipping, allowing for the possibility of coal export. The waggonway was constructed at a cost of £3,500, yet another significant investment on top of the already huge sum already paid. A local wright, William Dickson, was employed to fabricate, assemble, develop and repair the track and waggons, an arrangement which lasted at least twenty-three years.

By 1733, the York Buildings Company was in serious debt. Slow communication due to the distance from London made managing the Scottish estates extremely difficult. The company could no longer pay its employees' wages and many investors had been reduced to absolute poverty due to poor returns, forcing the company to begin selling off its assets. A variety of schemes and tactics were used to raise additional funds, including lotteries where the prizes on offer were shares in the company. These unethical methods were in vain, however, and over the next few decades the fortunes of the York Buildings Company continued to decline. Finally, in 1779, the Winton Estate was broken up into lots and sold off.

Construction by William Dickson

In 1722, the lands between Tranent and Cockenzie were a marsh, presenting a natural barrier in transporting coal to Port Seton Harbour, 2 miles away on the coast. The boggy ground, marked on early maps as a 'morass', made building and maintaining an effective transport route extremely difficult.

The 2½-mile-long waggonway was constructed from wood, possibly initially oak, as mentioned in the 'deed of tack' for tacksman Archibald Robertson in 1736. Under Scottish law, a 'tacksman' was a landholder who held a lease and sub-let their land to others. The track rested on a raft of round timbers which would help stabilise the track as it lay on the marsh. At the southern end, it took a route up 'The Heugh', a historic coal gorge which had been surface-worked for centuries, to a pit some quarter of a mile south of the post road.

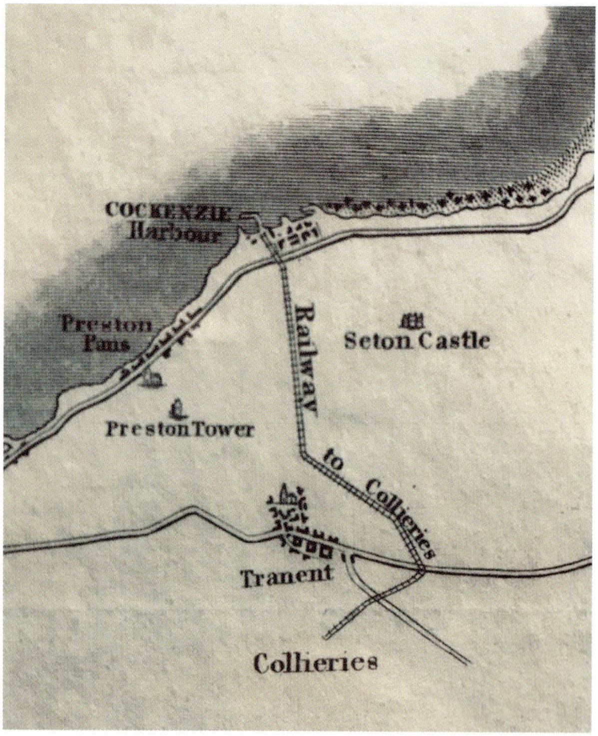

A nineteenth-century map of the Tranent–Cockenzie Waggonway by John Gellatly. (From an original in the authors' collection)

Above left: Local wright William Dickson building latrines prior to the construction of the waggonway in 1722. (Illustration by Alan Braby)

Above right: The first wooden waggonway under construction at Tranent. This waggonway was made up of a 'corduroy' of timber sleepers which helped with stability on wet, soft and boggy ground. (Illustration by Alan Braby)

At the northern end, it terminated at Port Seton Harbour after passing by and serving the salt pans at Cockenzie.

Much of the known information about the construction is down to the work journals of local wright William Dickson, who also mentions frequent use of 'ocktembear', or 'oak timber'. His record of the work he undertook from 1717–45 provides a unique and contemporary account of the initial construction, followed by subsequent repairs in three distinct phases of work. Notably, these separate phases of work all take place under three different leaseholders: Thomas Mathie, William Adam, and Francis Grant and Captain William Burrows.

However, interpretation of this documentary evidence has been enhanced through comparison with the archaeological findings of the 1722 Waggonway Project excavations in 2019 and 2021. Whilst Dickson does not mention the gauge of the waggonway, the archaeological evidence suggests it was 4 ft 0 in from an early stage. There does appear to have been an initial track consisting of a timber boardwalk with rails attached, but it is possible that this was used purely for moving materials while constructing the more robust 4-ft gauge track.

Dickson's first phase of activity begins on 7 May 1722, when he begins 'maken at the realls', a contemporary Scots spelling of 'making at the rails'. He spends at least two weeks

Above: A reconstructed horse gin at Beamish Museum. Similar machines were in use at Tranent during the eighteenth century. (John New)

Below: A replica of a typical chauldron waggon at Beamish Museum. (John New)

Above: A horse and replica waggon at Beamish Museum. (Paul Jarman)

Right: The replica wooden waggonway at Beamish Museum. (John New)

constructing rails before moving on to other tasks such as 'worken at the wagonway' and 'maken wagon wheealls'. This period of activity is fairly intense, and Dickson spends little time doing anything else other than waggonway-related work. It should be noted that Dickson could not have done all of this alone, and it is perhaps telling that in the weeks leading up to commencement of construction, he spends his time building 'leatrens', or 'latrines', an essential facility required for a labour force on a major project such as he was undertaking.

The activity noted by Dickson throughout the journals shows much 'mendin' and 'repearin' of the waggonway, hinting at a structure which was at the mercy of significant damage through wear and tear and the elements. In short, it required almost continuous repair. It is certainly significant that some periods of activity take place over two to three years, with weeks and months at a time devoted to jobs such as travelling to Fife for waggon wheels and journeying to estates around the county of Haddingtonshire, now East Lothian, for suitable timber 'for ows [use] of the wagonway'.

William Adam and Archibald Robertson

On 29 August 1727, William Adam signed an agreement with the York Buildings Company granting him the tenancy of the coal and salt works at Tranent and Cockenzie for twelve years. There was the option to terminate the agreement at the end of each three years, which Adam decided to do after nine years. He notified the York Buildings Company in March 1736.

William Adam, *c.* 1723, painted by William Aikman. (Wikimedia Commons)

Adam's decision gave rise to a large bundle of legal documents resulting from various hearings. Initially, the York Buildings Company went to court to ask that a 'roup' (auction) of the tenancy should be held in a legal setting, saying that they could not let it privately. The court agreed and set a date for the auction but then, in typical York Buildings Company fashion, they did a private deal and let it to a Francis Grant.

There were further legal arguments culminating in the decision that a roup should take place as legally agreed. It was advertised in the *Caledonian Mercury* on 26 August 1736 as due to take place on 9 September 1736. However, it actually happened on 28 September when the winning bid was placed by a John Baird. It then transpired that John Baird was acting on behalf of Archibald Robertson and the five-year tenancy was duly transferred to Robertson on 15 October 1736. He agreed to pay £460 sterling annually, and there is a lengthy document setting out the conditions he had to meet. These conditions included care of the waggonway:

> That whatever method is taken for carrying down the coals from the coal pitts to the salt works The Tacksman oblige himself to leave the waggon way waggons and Trunks at the pans in as good condition at the end of the tack as they are at his entry thereto with no less quantity of oak timber than is now contained in them. And particularly that he be obliged to keep and leave not only the timber of the waggon way but also the breadth of the earthen road on both sides of the way which supports the timber sleepers and raills and at the narrowest place to keep and leave them two foot of well rammed earth on each side of the raills of the said waggon road.

Archibald Robertson is described in a document dated 22 May 1735 as 'Coallmaster in Tranent', so it appears that he was working for William Adam, who also happened to be his brother-in-law, at the time he took over the tenancy of the Tranent and Cockenzie coal and salt works from him.

These legal arguments and devious dealings were typical of the York Buildings Company operations, and it is interesting that Archibald Robertson's identity was concealed until after the deal was done.

Eighteenth-Century Tenants and Owners

From its inception, this waggonway had several different tenants, perhaps hinting at the difficulty in turning a profit from such industries.

York Buildings Company (Owners)

- Thomas Mathie, merchant (1722–27)
- William Adam, entrepreneur and architect (1727–36)
- Archibald Robertson, coalmaster (1736–43)
- Francis Grant, merchant and Captain William Burrows, York Buildings Company agent (1743–59)
- William Cadell, merchant and industrialist (1759–77)

The Battle of Prestonpans (1745)

The Tranent–Cockenzie Waggonway, as early railways go, was fairly long-lived and as a result played host to an event that would shape the course of the nation's history.

On the early morning of 21 September 1745, the Hanoverian Army of King George faced the Jacobite Army of Bonnie Prince Charlie. Following a few days of manoeuvres, the two sides lined up in the fields between Preston and Seton.

The British artillery initially lined up roughly along a section of the waggonway. The track did not sit on a significant raised banking so provided little means of cover, rather serving primarily as a marker to line up against. Ultimately, the Jacobites were victorious following a successful charge across the open ground to the east, with several hundred Hanoverians killed during the rout which carried them back across the waggonway.

This action saw the battle become the first in history fought across a railway, but being the only direct route between Tranent and the lower ground, the waggonway also played a key role in the pre- and post-battle events. Prior to the battle a senior customs official, Walter Grosset, was sent up the line by the Hanoverian General John Cope to scope out the Jacobite positions. He was shot at for his troubles. Following the battle, it is the only route that the wounded Colonel Gardiner could have been taken from the field to Tranent Manse, where he famously perished in an upstairs room.

The day before the Battle of Prestonpans, 1745. The waggonway was central to the battlefield landscape, and played a part in movement of personnel before and after the battle. (Illustration by Alan Braby)

A New Era – the Cadell Family

The first significant records of the Cadell family of Cockenzie date from the beginning of the eighteenth century when a William Cadell is noted as living in Haddington working as a glazier and merchant. The family eventually settled in Cockenzie and ran a successful manufactory selling scythes, knives and similar items.

In 1750, William also oversaw the local construction of an impressively sized 'herring buss', a type of fishing vessel, called *The Grant*. This was captured nine years later by French privateers whilst sailing between Gothenburg and Cockenzie. From 1759, William took on the lease of the Tranent coal mines and Cockenzie salt works from the York Buildings Company, the latest in a string of tenants who had all tried, and largely failed, to make a decent profit from them.

The Cadells did, however, have greater good fortune than those who had come before them, and through their various ventures became prosperous industrialists branching out into many new enterprises. One of these was the Carron Iron Works in Falkirk which went on to forge fine-quality cannons, 'carronades', which were widely used in conflicts from the late eighteenth century to the mid-nineteenth century.

In 1777, William Cadell died and a short time later, in 1779, his son John purchased the waggonway, coal pits, salt works, Cockenzie House and surrounding land as a group following the liquidation of the York Buildings Company in 1777. Notably, this auction had very specific lots, with the one in question containing only the industrial package apparently

Above left: Cockenzie Harbour photographed by General Sir Robert Cadell, *c.* 1854. Waggonway lines can be seen in the foreground and an empty waggon and horse on the right. (Cockenzie House & Gardens)

Above right: Hew Francis Cadell (1790–1873). In 1829, he commissioned Robert Stevenson to design a new harbour at Cockenzie, which was completed in 1835. The existing waggonway was incorporated into the new quaysides. (Cockenzie House & Gardens)

being referred to as 'Cadell's Lot' at the time, indicating that there was a pre-agreed or desired outcome for the parcels of land in question. The bill of sale stated that:

> There is still an extensive field of coal, whereof no part has hitherto been wrought by fire engine or other proper machinery. The whole of the coal lies at a small distance from the sea. The port and harbour of Seaton make part of the estate to be sold; and there is a waggon-way from the coal-pits to the salt-pans and the shore.
>
> The waggon-way is to be communicated to the purchasers in Lots 2d and 3d of Tranent, and a liberty reserved, on paying damages, to carry the waggon-way through the links of Seaton to the harbour of Port-Seaton, in the direction it formerly went, when the coal was wrought for the Company's account.

Research by the 1722 Waggonway Project has uncovered local title deeds written by the Cadells in the mid-nineteenth century which describe the boundaries of the land in question using the route of the 'old waggonway' as a reference point. This has confirmed the route of the original waggonway in Cockenzie as what is now School Lane, which leads it towards what used to be Port Seton Links and the Port Seton Harbour area.

As significant landowners, the influence of the family grew and they became integral to life and work in the area. By 1810, the Cadells had modernised the old salt works, with John's son Hew Francis overseeing the work. Brick-built 'brander' furnaces with iron grates, ash-pits and flue systems were built, providing greater efficiency and further increasing the quality and quantity of salt produced.

James Paterson

In 1762, the first recorded death on this waggonway, or any in Scotland for that matter, occurred at Cockenzie. Local boy James Paterson's father, George, worked as a blacksmith in Cockenzie, close to the waggonway. It is unclear if eleven-year-old James was working on the waggonway or playing nearby, but on 27 August 1762 he was struck by a waggon, recorded as being 'bruised' in the local parish mortality book. He died from his injuries and was buried in Tranent kirkyard the next day. Incidentally, James Paterson senior was blacksmith at Cockenzie when William Dickson first began constructing the waggonway some forty years earlier.

From Wood to Iron

By 1815, the wooden waggonway was no longer fit for purpose. Wear and tear meant that the worn-out timbers needed almost constant repair. Hew Francis Cadell replaced the waggonway with cast-iron 'fish-belly' rails, sitting on stone sleeper blocks. This incarnation of the waggonway, however, took a slightly different route, running to what remained of the old seventeenth-century Cockenzie Harbour en route to the salt pans, as some five years earlier Port Seton Harbour had been significantly damaged by a storm and was seemingly unusable.

Fish-belly rail fragments, iron chairs and stone sleepers at the 1722 Waggonway Heritage Centre. These have been recovered from archaeological digs and local gardens since 2017.

The gauge of the new track was 3 ft 3 in, with the fish-belly rails held in place by iron chairs secured to the stone sleeper blocks with iron pins driven into wooden dowels. The waggons were also redesigned, incorporating more cast- and wrought-iron features, most notably the wheels. Once fully loaded, four waggons coupled together formed a small train. The mode of descent did not change, however, and gravity and a brakesman was still required, with photographs taken by General Sir Robert Cadell in the 1850s showing a clear image of the waggons in use at Cockenzie Harbour.

Alexander Scott, in 1824, described the waggonway as follows:

> Mr Cadell's waggons travel from his coal-works, in Tranent Moor, to Cockenzie, a distance of upwards of 4,480 yards, on a cast-iron railway, that has various declivities and circular turns; and require only the assistance of a man, in the downward journey, to attend to the several brakes attached to the waggons. The breadth of the horse-track is 3 feet 3 inches; the waggons, when loaded, including their carriages, are each about 2 tons. A horse sometimes takes up 5 empty waggons, but the common number is 4, and these he commonly drags three times a day.

Scott describes a busy operation; a thriving railway system in which each horse and train make three round trips a day.

A New Harbour – Robert Stevenson

The improvements to the salt works and waggonway sparked an increase in exports. As a result, in 1829, the Cadells commissioned renowned civil engineer Robert Stevenson to produce designs for the expansion of Cockenzie Harbour. To allow larger ships to berth, a

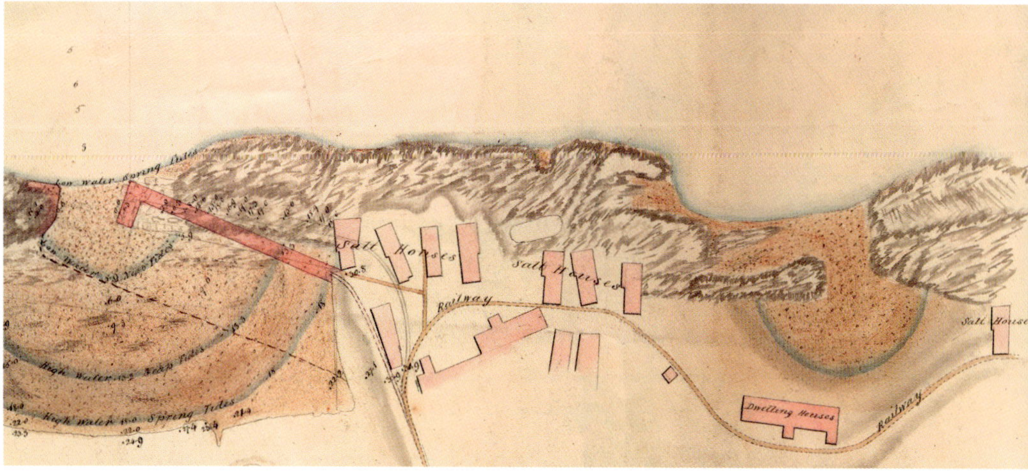

A detail from an 1829 sketch plan of Cockenzie by Robert Stevenson & Sons, showing an early proposal for a new harbour. Note the light-pink salt houses served by waggonway sidings coloured in brown. Proposed features are marked in dark pink and pencil line. (Stevenson Collection; reproduced with the permission of the National Library of Scotland)

new eastern pier was proposed along with excavation of rock from the harbour seabed. The plans also proposed a system of innovative waggonway turntables and 'tilting apparatus' which allowed coals to be loaded directly into the holds of ships via moveable chutes.

The relationship between Hew Francis Cadell and Robert Stevenson appears to have been very close, with much of Stevenson's end of the correspondence surviving in his letter books. In particular, he feels confident enough to invite himself to breakfast on one occasion and was even presented with a commemorative quaich made from the wood of The Thorntree, of Battle of Prestonpans fame, beneath which Colonel Gardiner was mortally wounded on 21 September 1745.

A detail from an 1841 sketch plan of Cockenzie Harbour by Robert Stevenson & Sons, showing existing waggonway lines and turntables on the quayside at Cockenzie Harbour. Note the coal drop marks next to each turntable, and Mr Cadell's Office overseeing the harbour area. (Stevenson Collection; reproduced with the permission of the National Library of Scotland)

Cockenzie Harbour, showing waggons and coal drop gantries, *c.* 1854. (Cockenzie House & Gardens)

Following several years of evaluation, surveying and planning, the foundation stone of the harbour was laid on 19 July 1833 and construction was completed in 1835 with the total cost being £6,000. Around this time, the waggonway route was also extended to the eastern side of Tranent to new coal pits in the Windygoul area.

The harbour was advertised in the local press, with an article in the *Caledonian Mercury* referring to it as a 'commodious haven' capable of berthing all manner of craft and leading the reader to believe that this was the new place to do business and shipping. In 1841, Robert Stevenson was contracted once again to draw up plans for a remodelling of the southern side of the harbour, with a new quayside and 'lady's stairs' proposed. These plans were never completed, however, with the harbour today being unchanged since the 1833 modifications.

Archaeology

The Tranent–Cockenzie Waggonway has been extensively explored through archaeological excavation, largely due to the work of the 1722 Waggonway Project, a community-led organisation which is dedicated to furthering the knowledge of this line and its associated industries.

Cockenzie Harbour

Between 2017 and 2023, a significant number of surviving in situ features of the nineteenth-century waggonway infrastructure were discovered.

An artist's impression of Cockenzie Harbour in the mid-nineteenth century showing salt pans and the waggonway lines on the quayside. (Illustration by Alan Braby)

Along the eastern quayside, remains of two 3-ft gauge sidings were uncovered. Running along the eastern pier itself, a row of stone sleeper blocks is incorporated into the fabric of the quayside working surface. This line is shown on the 1841 Stevenson plan. Some of the blocks still retained the rusted remains of iron chairs set into rebates in the surface. Additionally, this siding had the remains of turntable and tilting apparatus used to unload coal from the waggonway into ships in the harbour below. The tilting apparatus remains exactly match the plans made by Robert Stevenson for a 'tilting apparatus used at Cockenzie'. Correspondence between Stevenson and H. F. Cadell indicate that this was a device already in use at Cockenzie, rather than one of the engineer's own designs.

To the north-east, another linked siding was partially examined in 2017, and then more extensively excavated in 2023. This revealed a double row of eight stone sleeper blocks, regularly spaced at approximately 3-ft intervals, being the length of the cast-iron rails in use. The gauge was 3 ft 3 in between rail centres, suggesting a gauge between the gauge faces of the rails of 3 ft. A thin layer of rammed, compacted small coal and industrial waste was laid as a roadbed onto which the stone blocks were directly laid, with packing stones around them. Further tips of rammed small coal and industrial waste formed the ballast to hold the sleeper blocks in place, with the ballast lapping over the top of the stones.

The chairs to support the ends of the rails were cast iron, with two holes to take pins to secure them to the stone block. They are relatively simple castings, to receive the butt-ends of two sections of rail, secured by a common key which slid into a cast rebate or socket on

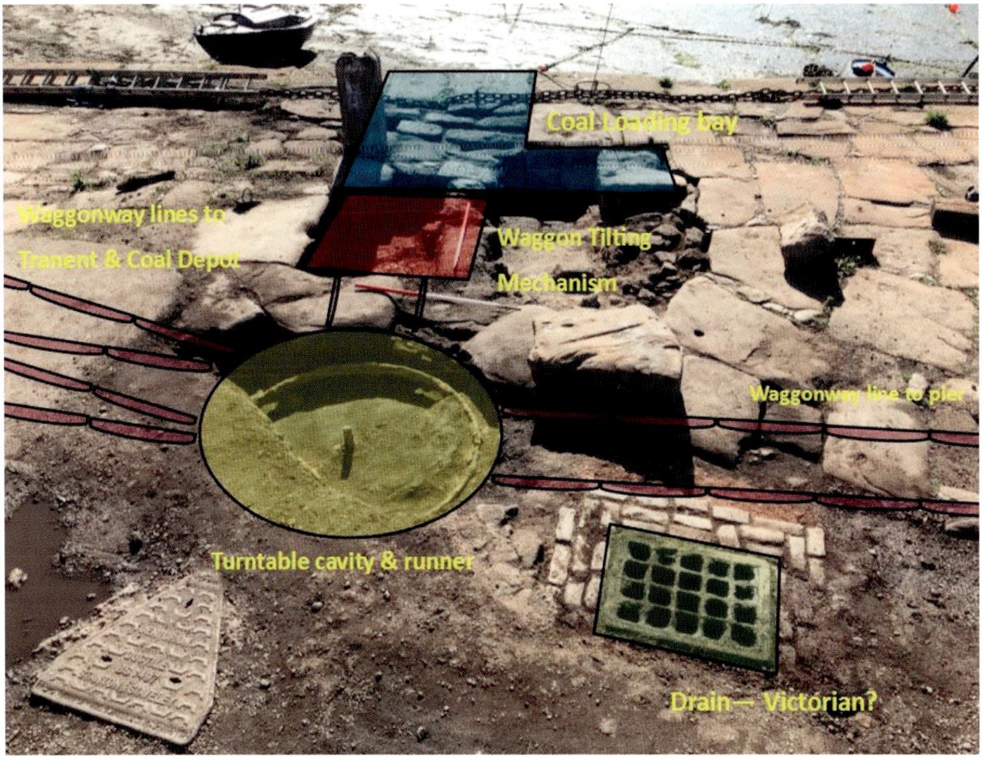

During 2018, the turntable and coal tipper area at Cockenzie Harbour were excavated by the 1722 Waggonway Project. Much of the foundation infrastructure remained in situ.

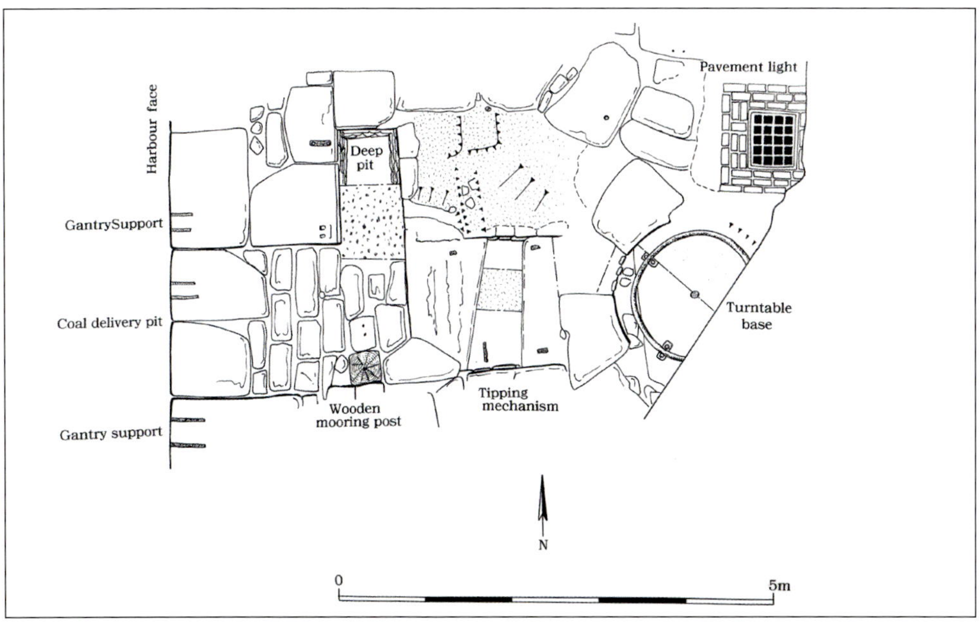

An archaeological plan of the turntable and tipper area at Cockenzie. (Alan Braby)

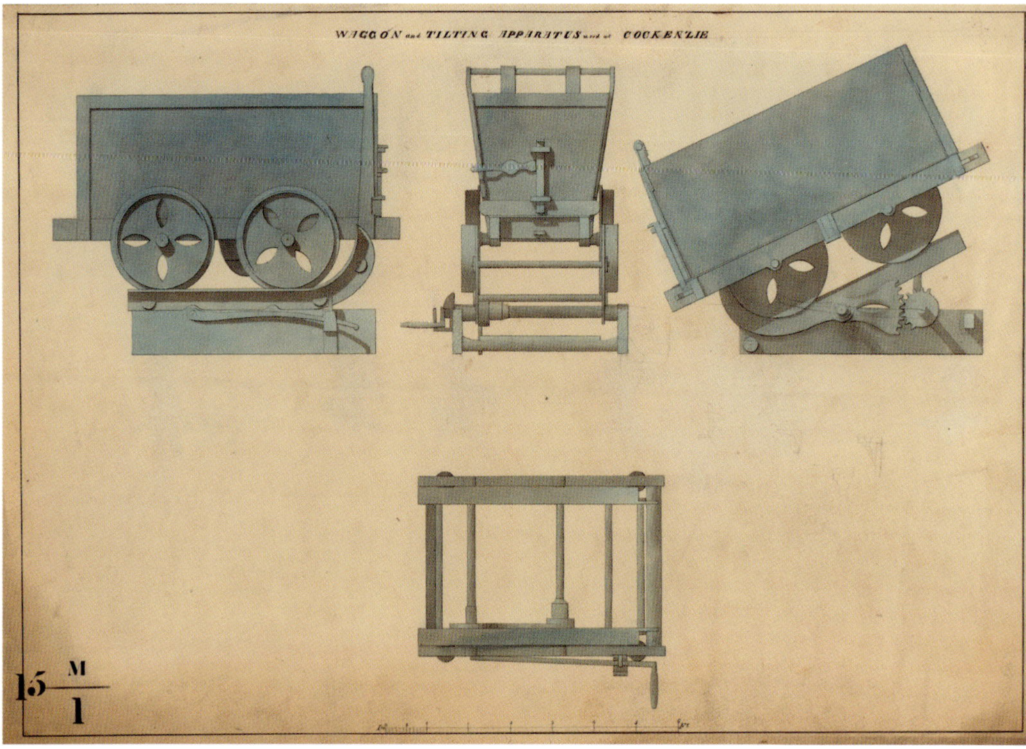

Above: A waggon and tilting apparatus used at Cockenzie, as illustrated by Robert Stevenson. This device allowed coal to be deposited via a door at the end of the waggon. Surviving correspondence between Stevenson and H. F. Cadell indicates that this machine was already in use at Cockenzie and that Stevenson wanted to copy and install it at future harbour projects. (Stevenson Collection; reproduced with the permission of the National Library of Scotland)

Left: Stone sleepers at Cockenzie Harbour, uncovered during the 2017 excavation.

In situ cast-iron chair discovered during the 2017 excavation. Note that it had been packed around with clay as part of a repair.

A wooden sleeper used at Cockenzie to underpin the rails where 'slump' had occurred with the stone sleepers.

one side of the chair. The fit between the chair and the stone block appears to have been poor; but this is also true of examples of the Liverpool & Manchester Railway.

One large fragment of cast-iron fish-belly rail has been recovered archaeologically. It has a simple T-shaped profile and includes a small, lower flange which dates the rail to after around 1811. This fits with the generally accepted date of 1815, or perhaps slightly later of 1818, for the laying of this upgrade of the waggonway, given the probable involvement of Robert Stevenson, who was championing the principle of the iron railway at the time.

Evidence from 2023 demonstrates that considerable difficulty was experienced in forming a true curve. Instead, the curves were polygonal, formed from individual straight sections of track 3-ft long, angled in their chair to form a rough curve. This would have presented a considerable problem in ensuring that both the inner and outer radii were the same. The fixed lengths of the rails meant that staggered joints had to be used to create a curve.

This section of stone-sleepered track provides useful evidence for the laying out and construction of curves using short sections of cast-iron rails. The resulting curve is not a smooth transition, simply a series of short, straight lengths which would have necessitated slow speeds and light loads. It would also have required considerable maintenance to keep the curve true to gauge, as is evidenced by several patches and bodged repairs including pinning together of cracked and slumped stone blocks, the use of wood packing underneath chairs, and seemingly 'temporary fixes' of timbers underneath the centre of the fish-belly rails to create an 'intermediate chair' or even replacement of a broken stone block completely. Various cuts and recuts of stone holes at the harbour end are further evidence of these running repairs.

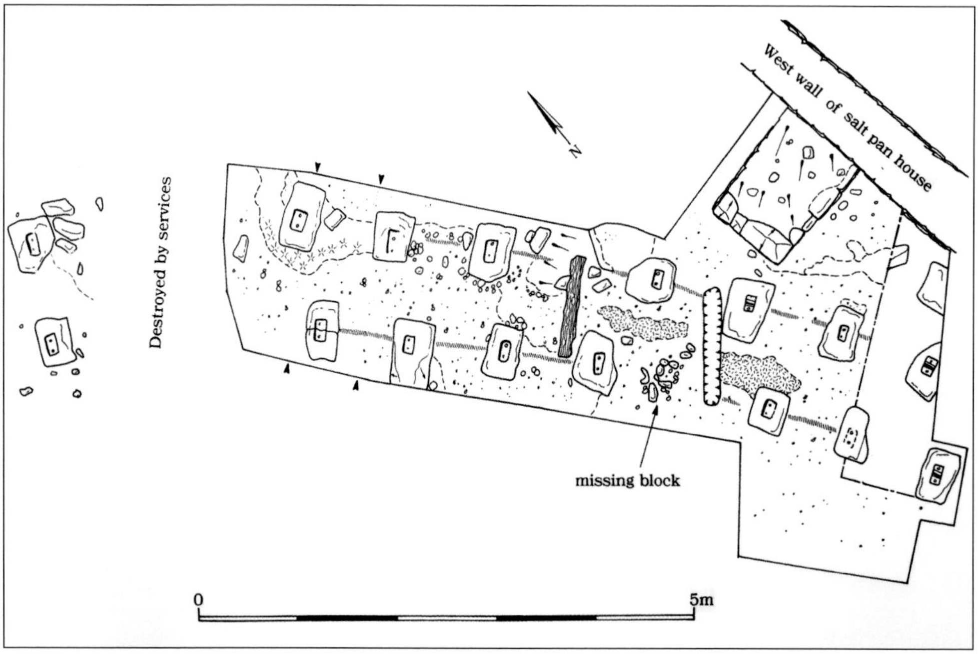

An archaeological plan of a waggonway siding at Cockenzie Harbour. (Alan Braby)

Cockenzie Coalfauld

The area immediately to the south of Cockenzie Harbour is known as the 'coalfauld', or the 'Coal Depot', as shown on the 1841 Cockenzie Harbour plans by Robert Stevenson & Sons.

In 2022, excavations of an area near the entrance of the compound, now a car yard, revealed that more significant infrastructure survived within than was previously thought. Indeed, some structures which were not marked on any maps were found, specifically a raised embankment with a battered stone face supporting the base of a tilting apparatus like that found at the nearby harbour. Coal was being unloaded from this embankment to a yard area with a large opening to the main Edinburgh Road on the northern side, indicating that this was a 'landsale wharf', an area where coal could be sold to the public rather than industry.

There were also hints of an earlier wooden structure beneath the nineteenth-century remains.

The coal drop at Cockenzie Coalfauld under excavation in 2022. This structure supported a waggon-tilting apparatus, as seen at nearby Cockenzie Harbour.

A model showing the coalfauld at Cockenzie. Note the split level and coal drop. (Model by Alan Braby)

Waggonway Route at Prestonpans Battlefield

The excavations in 2019 and 2021 form some of the most important railway archaeology undertaken nationally to date. Discovered at a depth of 1 m, the remains of the earliest wooden waggonway were found under the eastern side of the current footpath which follows the route of the Tranent–Cockenzie Waggonway where it crosses the site of the 1745 Battle of Prestonpans.

Predominantly mineralised rail timbers at a gauge of 4 ft flanked a cobbled walking surface, topped with industrial slag-rich furnace waste and a small-coal upper layer packed down to a solid crust. Robust wooden sleepers underpinned the rails and evidence was found in a section of double rails, with an upper replaceable one resting on top of a lower one. However, immediately underneath this structure, there was evidence of a much simpler structure constructed in the form of a corduroy of timbers with rails of an unknown gauge. This could either be the quickly replaced first waggonway, or an access railway used for moving materials during the construction of the 4-ft gauge waggonway. Amongst the material used to make the horse track was glass-slag from the nearby Port Seton Glassworks, which was in operation from 1728–36, while pottery (Cadell and Roebuck barleycorn pattern plate) dating to around the 1750s was found upon the uppermost small-coal surface. Whilst the glass-slag may not be diagnostic, the pottery certainly is, suggesting a link with either Dickson's final phase of work in 1744 or a hitherto unrecorded phase initiated by the Cadells.

The 2021 excavation of the Tranent–Cockenzie Waggonway, north of Meadowmill. The cobbled horse track is covered in small coal and the imprints of wooden rails and sleepers are visible.

Above: The imprint of sleepers shown underlying the cobbles of the horse track.

Right: Some of the rails and sleepers excavated were mineralised to a solid state.

The wooden waggonway does not sit centrally to the modern-day path, as had been assumed, but on the eastern side. Immediately to the west of the waggonway the hints of another line were found, indicating that this could have been a passing place on the line. On either side of the routeway evidence was found of small ditches at field level, which would have helped with drainage.

The design of this waggonway structure is comparable to that of Willington, excavated in 2013, and provides some style links with waggonways in the north-east of England, albeit this structure predates Willington by some forty to sixty years. The importance of this waggonway in archaeological terms is second to none, as it gives the clearest snapshot of how the earliest railway in Scotland was put together.

Of the later 1815 iron waggonway, which replaced the original wooden construction, no trace was found save some broken fish-belly rail and iron chair fragments in the spoil.

Experimental Archaeology

Recent experiments to recreate a section of the Tranent–Cockenzie Waggonway have been conducted, with a 20-ft stretch of track being built by volunteers from the 1722 Waggonway Project.

The goal was to use the archaeological evidence from the 2019 and 2021 excavations to faithfully recreate the track, whilst gaining valuable experiential knowledge and data

Sawing sleepers for the replica waggonway using period attire and tools.

Trenails were crafted by hand and used to peg the rails and sleepers together.

to assist with future plans for a larger-scale reconstruction. Of particular note was the discovery that small timbers inserted between the upper rails had the purpose of providing extra lateral support, thus adding durability and support under the load of a loaded coal waggon. Period costume was worn throughout the process and as many of the components as possible were made by hand.

A team of six members of the Waggonway Heritage Group was able to build two 3-m lengths of replica wooden waggonway over two six- to seven-hour working days. The first example was single rail, with the rails laid on half round timbers. This was a very simple method of construction. The rails would have been prepared off-site where there would have been access to a saw pit, probably in Dickson's own timber yard in Cockenzie. They were then transported to site, using the wooden corduroy and along the waggonway as it extended from Cockenzie to Tranent. The sleepers were branches felled from trees with the bark left on. It was very simple to prepare two level sections on each sleeper to receive the rail. These were then drilled with a brace and bit and secured together with a wooden trenail. Very few metal tools would have been needed on the worksite other than a drill, hatchet and adze.

The 'double way' railway with two rails stacked on top of each other was more complicated to build, requiring more carpentry work but there was nothing new or unique

Above: The experimental archaeology team wore period costume and prepared all components by hand to capture the most accurate information possible.

Left: A member of the reconstruction team drilling holes for trenails.

The 1722 Waggonway Project's replica coal waggon on the new experimental section of waggonway.

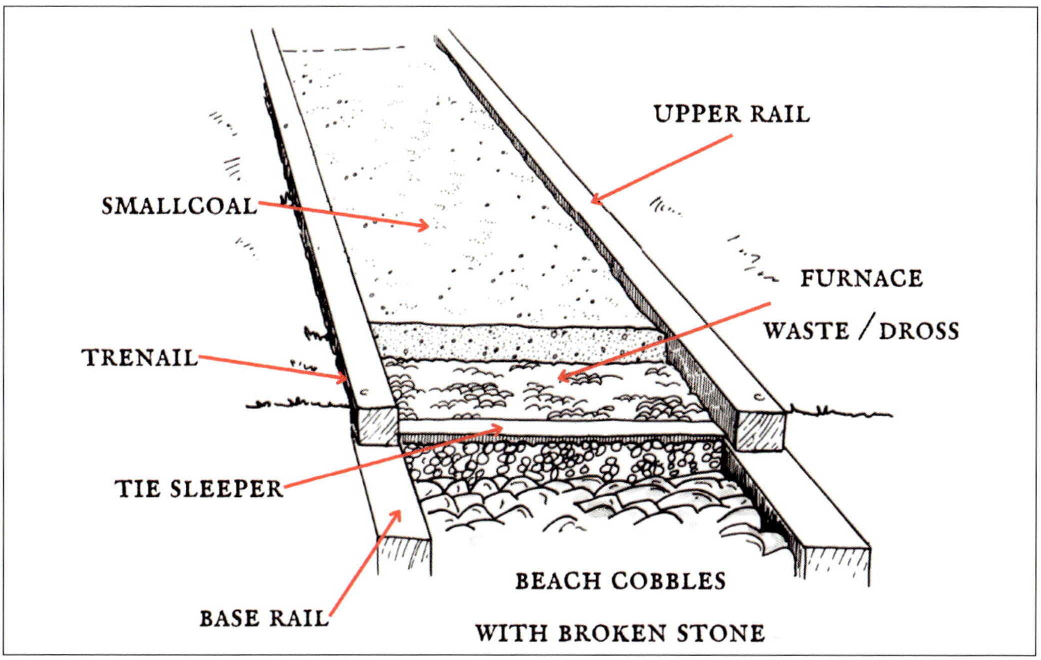

An illustration of the waggonway design used at Cockenzie, based on the archaeological findings from excavations in 2019 and 2021.

An illustration of a nineteenth-century waggon from the Tranent–Cockenzie Waggonway. This features excellent detail and is comparable with waggons seen in photographs from the 1850s.

about the process. The rails and sleepers were jointed together using half-lap joints, secured with trenails: half-lap joints are easy to make and one of the first joints taught to trainee joiners. Again, components were likely prepared off-site, where each track section was dry-assembled, dismantled and re-erected on-site, exactly as timber-framed buildings were in the period. From this data it was proposed that a similar-sized team of trained and skilled joiners would have been able to build 1 km of such a waggonway in twenty-eight days, suggesting it would have only taken 112 days (or just over three months) to build the entire waggonway.

CHAPTER 2

The First Waggonways

It is worth noting when looking at the growth and development of wooden waggonways across Scotland that these lines were often fairly temporary, and if they lasted any decent length of time, they required significant repair and maintenance. When examining just some of the early waggonways of the eighteenth century, it is not just the general evolutionary beginnings of early railways that can be understood, but also the development of these lines in their own local contexts.

Wooden waggonways were easy to rebuild, reroute and extend as need dictated, as seen at Tranent with the addition of a southeastern spur to new coal pits to the east of the town. However, some did last longer, as with both Tranent–Cockenzie and Fordell, both of which were upgraded and developed between the eighteenth and twentieth centuries.

All of the early wooden waggonways served industry, with coal being brought from the pits to salt works, glass works, brick works and for export. Salt in particular offered a use for the poorer-quality coal, and in Brora there are echoes of East Lothian's portfolio of furnace-based processes.

The Far North – Brora

Brora is a long way from East Lothian. It's a long way from most places, for that matter. Tucked away in the relative wilds of Sutherland, this town is another whose history has been dictated by its natural resources and the industrial opportunities which they presented. Again, we see the availability of coal to a coast where it is possible to collect brine, shaping an industrial centre which was integral to life in the area for several centuries.

The coal in this area comes from Jurassic geology and was mined extensively for around 400 years from Britain's northernmost coal mine, fuelling the fires of the industrial centre. The first salt works was established at the end of the sixteenth century when, in 1598, Lady Jean Gordon, Countess of Sutherland, introduced the first salt works. This first venture into saltmaking in Brora continued until 1617. After a lengthy hiatus the industry was revived here in 1767, again lasting for just a brief ten years. However, during this second phase of saltmaking, the first waggonway was constructed here, with a wooden railway introduced

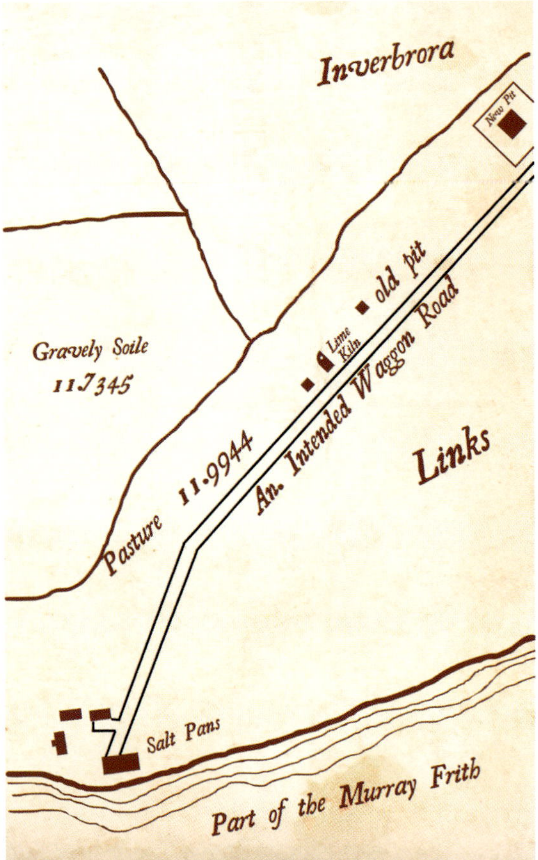

A copy of a detail from John Kirk's 'Survey of Farms in Golspie and Loth Parishes, Sutherland, circa 1772', showing a possible route for the waggonway in Brora. The 'Intended Waggon Road' runs past both old and new coal pits to the salt pans. (Ed Bethune)

to serve the coal and salt operations. Salt manufacture returned from 1812–28 but again did not succeed.

Clearly, the making of salt was fraught with difficulties in this location, and even today the shifting dunes and eroding coastline is clear to see. The exposed nature of the coast, facing directly and unprotected onto the North Sea, was the bane of the industrialists who tried and tried again to make it work.

Despite the difficulties, however, industry did survive in Brora. Extensive brick and tile manufacturing was also established in the area, beginning in 1814 and again with some lengthy gaps in operation, ultimately lasting until the 1970s.

The story of the waggonways in Brora is a fairly typical one, with an initial 1-mile wooden line of a very narrow 1 ft 8 in being constructed by a John Williams in the 1770s, although the exact date is unclear. There then followed a similar evolution to many of these early railways, as lines were added and removed as required.

A map by John Kirk dated 1772 is helpful in showing the extent of the coal pits to the south of Brora at that time and helpfully shows 'An Intended Waggon Road' running from the harbour to the salt pans, past the old and new coal pits. It is worth noting that the terminology 'waggon road' has been used in verifiable cartographical context at Tranent, on Forrest's map of 1799, to indicate a waggonway. The salt pans in question have been

An archaeological trench cut across the 'intended waggonroad' at Brora, Sutherland. A layer of pan scratch (salt pan waste) from the salt pan was used to form the horse track.

eroded by the sea, although in 2020 a joint archaeological team from Scape Trust, Clyne Heritage Society and the 1722 Waggonway Project excavated a test trench on the line of the possible 'waggon road'. Despite hints of a possible structure, the results of the evaluation were inconclusive; the remains of a routeway were found, but the shifting dunes and poor conditions for preservation had left no definitive answer to the question of whether a waggonway or waggon road was ever constructed here. It is at the very least a demonstration of the rarity of wooden railways being found in a recognisable and interpretable condition. Whether the 'Intended Waggon Road' is one and the same as Williams' one is as yet unproven.

In 1810, the Marquis of Stafford instigated development of the brick and tile works, necessitating an improved waggonway or tramway system. A new network of iron-edge-railed lines was the result, with these new lines following different routes to the old, including linking the Faskally pit to the north, via a bridge over the River Brora to the harbour.

However, to the south of the river another coal pit was also opened in the late eighteenth or early nineteenth century, and a large embankment was constructed to carry a waggonway line along the south side of the river to link up to the rest of the network in the town. Whether this pit was successfully operated is not wholly clear as records are scarce, but the absence of written documentation combined with the lack of coal waste in the immediate vicinity of the pit hints that perhaps that it was not fully finished.

Above: The surviving waggonway embankment at Brora is still a major feature in the landscape. However, despite its size, this section may never have been used.

Left: By the early twentieth century various industries at Brora were linked by a series of horse-drawn waggonways.

This small network of waggonway lines was partly abandoned by 1920, but elements continued to be used until 1947. Some remains of the iron railway survive built into local infrastructure, notably rails used as reinforcement in the icehouse at the harbour.

Wooden Railways Around the Firth of Forth

At a similar time, on the Forth Estuary, waggonways were by now all the rage, with several having popped up at various centres of industry: Leven (around 1760), of which little is known; Carron Works (around 1766), which was part of the Carron Iron Company and saw the extensive upgrading to be expected as part of such a cutting-edge industrial operation; and Berrylaw-Limekilns (around 1768), constructed by the 5th Earl of Elgin.

The **Alloa Waggonway** opened in 1766 as a purely wooden railway. As early as 1709 John Earl of Mar, the owner of the Alloa colliery, had sent his agent to Newcastle to inspect machinery and railways then in use, but this research trip seems to have come to naught as a railway wouldn't be constructed for another fifty years. The waggonway was built to carry coal from pits at Alloa to the Forth for onward shipping to Edinburgh but it also served a brewery, a distillery, a brick and tile works and finally the great Alloa Glassworks, which was 'to the west of the ferry, for making bottles... It can have any quantity of coals it requires, at a very easy rate.' The coal was 'conveyed from the pits, to the very doors of the glass house'. As it ran through Alloa, the waggonway went beneath Bedford Place through what is the oldest railway tunnel in Scotland. The wagons were pulled by horses on up-hill and level stretches and allowed to run downhill under gravity. One newspaper report describes how the overworked horses were 'in a miserable condition, and shamefully used'.

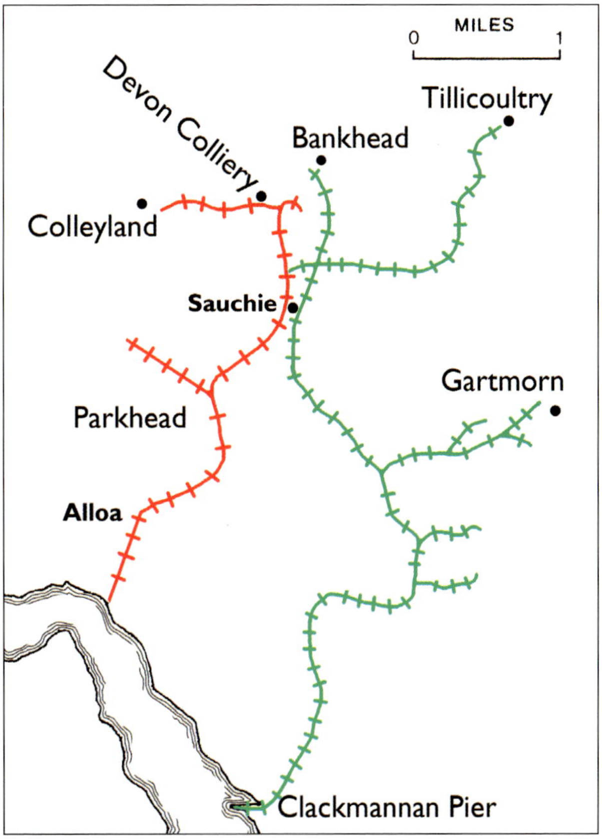

A map of the Alloa Waggonway and its neighbouring Sauchie Waggonway of 1806. The Sauchie provided an alternative route for coals mined at Collyland and Tillicoultry including to Clackmannan Pier for onward travel by sea. (Anthony Dawson)

The drivers often beat their charges so hard as to cause open wounds; many of them had sores on their necks and shoulders where their collars and tack had rubbed the skin raw. In 1855, several of the Alloa drivers were taken to court and fined for cruelty to animals. One notorious case featured a driver feeding horses whiskey to keep them going for longer without a rest!

The waggonway was laid to a gauge of 3 ft 3 in and used end-tipping wagons which were capable of carrying one Scots Chalder of coal (30 long cwt). According to Sir John Sinclair writing in 1796, the track was at first laid with Scotch pine rails and sleepers, the rails being about 5 in by 4 in, but this wore so badly that a second rail was soon affixed on top – a pattern seen on the Tranent–Cockenzie Waggonway, and south of the border. The use of soft wood rails was not a success either and they were soon changed for beech, a close-grained hard wood that wore much better and with use became smooth and glossy and thus relatively free of friction.

The line was extended to Collyland in 1771 but by 1785 this original wooden railway was completely worn out and the railway was rebuilt, including iron strap rails. These were 4 ft long and 1¼ in square – effectively a form of bar rail – and secured to the wooden rails with nails or screws through three projecting lugs. The wooden rails were double, i.e. one stacked on top of the other 'of best Memel or Prussian fir', 'fixed by wooden pins and

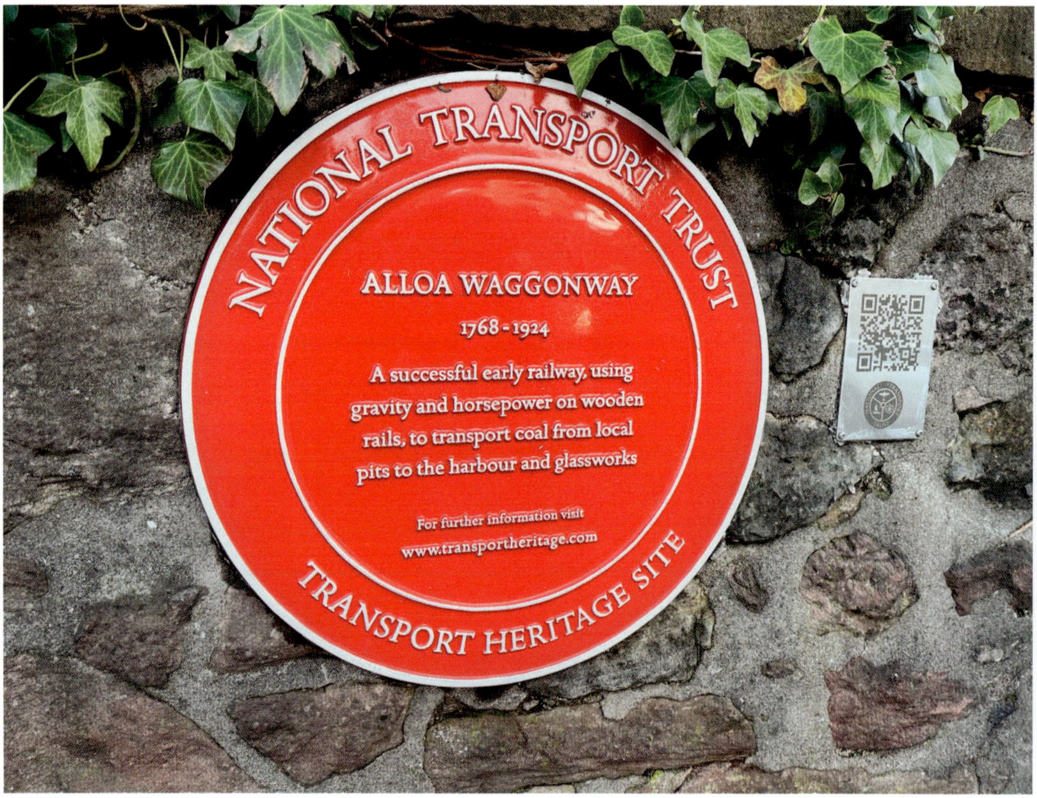

In March 2021, a red Transport Trust plaque was unveiled in Alloa to commemorate the waggonway and its importance in Scottish transport history. (Ed Bethune)

Right: The Alloa Waggonway ran through the streets of the town, including behind a school and close to many homes and gardens. It is seen here looking toward the Bedford Place tunnel. (Ed Bethune)

Below: The interior of the Bedford Place tunnel on the Alloa Waggonway – the earliest railway tunnel in Scotland. (Ed Bethune)

cross pieces'. Despite the cost, however: 'This plan proved quite abortive, for the instant the wood gave way or yielded, the cast iron was broken, and it was found so useless and expensive that it was thrown aside altogether...' (Lewis 1970: 265). Therefore, the railway had to be completely renewed:

> This was done on a new plan; and it is now acknowledged to be the most complete in Britain. The sleepers are very broad, and only 18 inches from centre to centre. A rail of foreign fir, 4 inches square, is pinned down to them, and another rail, of the same dimensions is laid over it, and the whole well beat up in good clay; on the top of the upper rail is laid a bar of malleable iron, of 1 ¾ inches breadth, and nearly six-8ths thick. (Dott 1947: 26)

The 'foreign fir' was likely imported from the Baltic, as was most of the timber used in Scotland.

These wrought-iron rails are described as being of Swedish iron, 1¾ in broad and ¾ in thick. The use of malleable, i.e. wrought, iron would have made the strap rails lighter and less brittle and thus less prone to fracture. In this form the Alloa Waggonway cost £800 per mile. The use of strap rails not only prolonged the life of the track but improved its efficiency. When the railway was entirely wooden, a horse could pull a single wagon loaded with 30 cwt of coal. Thanks to the lower rolling resistance from the strap rails, a

Coal tubs and interpretation boards have been placed in Alloa as reminders of the extensive coal trade and of the pioneering Alloa Waggonway. (Ed Bethune)

single horse could pull three wagons fitted with iron wheels, making a total load of 90 cwt. The line was built on a falling gradient from the coal pits so that: '1 horse draws 4½ tons of coal at once; and the declivity of the way is so gentle that the same horse draws with ease the 3 empty waggons back to the coal-hill.' Sinclair remarked that: 'The first expense of making this kind of waggonway is undoubtedly great', being at least 10*s.* per yard but had gone six years without 'any repair worth mentioning' and it was one of the finest in Britain.

Nearly a decade later, however, the wooden rails were so rotten and 'the repairs were never ending and expensive' it was rebuilt again, this time with cast-iron rails, in 1807. It was described as having cast-iron rails of a tall rectangular section spiked to wooden sleepers through holes cast into feet at either end, the rails having a dovetail end which socketed into each other like a jigsaw puzzle. The 'most extensive' iron railway is mentioned in the sale particulars of the Alloa Glassworks by the Edinburgh Glasshouse Company in 1812, which had 'afforded every convenience' to it. The line was re-laid again with wrought-iron fish-belly rail, secured with cast-iron chairs to stone sleeper blocks 5 in square. It was rebuilt again in 1840 with new wrought-iron rails.

The line ran through the oldest part of Alloa town, and despite being walled off it still ran in close proximity to the population. By the middle of the nineteenth century it had developed a reputation for being 'unfortunate' regarding the number of accidents. There were two in September 1856 alone. The five-year-old son of Alexander Gall was killed when he fell off a loaded waggon he had climbed aboard. Three-year-old James Robertson was killed by a waggon where the waggonway ran behind a row of houses, having left his mother's sight and had got onto the track behind their house. Matters were not helped as the line ran in a deep cutting only 4 ft away from the Parish School, resulting in several pupils being involved in accidents. In 1873, it was proposed to cover over the waggonway so as to 'safeguard against accidents' and to reroute the waggonway to also improve safety.

With the opening of a mainline railway in Alloa in 1851 the waggonway lost some of its importance, but it continued to operate carrying coal as it always had done, by horse and gravity, until finally closing in 1924.

One of the Alloa waggons survived after closure to be used as a coal bunker at the harbour. This photograph was taken by George Dott in the 1930s. (After George Dott)

Fordell Waggonway

Farther east in the Fife lands near Fordell House, built by the Henderson family in 1721, Sir Robert Henderson, 4th Baronet, in 1752 built a harbour which became known as St David's. He connected it by wooden railway not long after, possibly around 1769, to the coal pits to the north of Fordell Castle, which had been worked since the sixteenth century. It is shown on John Ainslie's map of 1775, so was certainly operational by then. As with other similar scenarios, this greatly increased the speed of coal transit to the coast, where again salt pans were served by the waggonway. The line was long and had multiple extensions, running at its greatest length up to 5¾ miles to serve many pits, notably Alice Pit and William Pit near Mossmorran, Big Mine at Prathouse and the Quarries near Fordell House.

The waggonway at Fordell was 4-ft gauge, and the waggons could carry 48 cwt; however, Robert Bald noted in 1817 that waggons were often overloaded, thus carrying greater loads and needing two horses to pull each waggon. One early Fordell waggon survives in the National Museums of Scotland stores. It was in 1817 that ownership passed to Admiral Sir Philip Durham, baronet, who was the son-in-law of Sir Robert.

The wooden line at Fordell was replaced by a malleable iron railway, with works being completed by 1838. This included a tunnel under the road between Crossgates and Donibristle, and a 332-yd self-acting incline where empty waggons would be pulled up by full ones descending, via a rope slung around a horizontal wheel at the top of the plane. A brake on this wheel allowed for a controlled descent. Another incline at Vantage was 1,148 yd with a gradient of 1:23.

After extensive engineering improvements to all aspects of the line, it eventually saw use as a steam railway from March 1868, with the suitably named 'St David's' being the first locomotive to run the newly re-laid steel rails. Around 1900, the Alice Pit yard was developed to include mixed gauge sidings, allowing the coal to be easily transferred to the standard gauge main line. Of all the early Scottish wooden railways, the development of this line shows the greatest modernisation through its lifespan.

A horse-drawn waggon on the Fordell Railway, photographed in the 1940s just prior to the closure of the railway. (After Dott)

Another view of a horse and waggon, showing the end door through which coal was discharged. (After Inglis & Inglis 1946)

Remarkably, one of the Fordell waggons survives and is preserved at the National Museum of Scotland, a unique survivor of Scotland's horse-drawn railways. (Graham Rule)

A lime kiln alongside the trackbed of the Halbeath Waggonway. (Bill Roberton)

The **Halbeath Waggonway**, near Dunfermline, was also established in the late eighteenth century, between 1780 and 1783. A similar length to Fordell, this line was conceived by the Lloyd brothers and engineered by Alexander Thompson. Shortly after, the line passed into the ownership of Campbell Morrison & Co. Ltd. The wooden rails were upgraded, likely with iron strips atop the wood around 1798 and subsequently by iron edge rail around 1811, thus following the timeline of its neighbouring line at Alloa.

The gauge of this waggonway is not known. However, as neighbouring lines were mostly around 4-ft wide and the waggons being known to hold around 42 cwt, it is probable that the gauge was similar to that of the nearby lines.

The railway saw many changes of route, again typical of these early lines, and by 1847 the Halbeath Colliery which gave the route its name was no longer connected to the line. Although a branch to Townhill and Appin collieries was successful, proposed links to Dunfermline and Charlestown, and separately Kirkaldy, failed to be completed.

The West of Scotland

Wooden waggonways were not confined to the east coast, however. The line at Knightswood, built by John Dixon (around 1750–75), served a glassworks that had been purchased by that early industrialist in 1750. At Ayr, in 1775, the Whitletts Colliery and Newton were both connected to Ayr Harbour.

Dr Lewis notes that the large waggon capacity (60 cwt) indicates that the design was probably based on Tyneside design rather than Shropshire. It would seem likely that the influence of Sunderland engineer Dixon had a part to play in this style of waggonway being prevalent in the west of Scotland. John and his son William, not to be confused with William Dickson of Cockenzie, had a significant role in many of the wooden railways in the Glasgow area during this period.

As ever with early wooden railways, exact dates and routes can be challenging to pin down, but certainly the network at Ayr served several coal pits between Newton, Auchincruive Holm and Ayr Harbour. At its most extensive, the lines here extended to a total of 2½ miles long and served not only the harbour with coal for export, but quarries, a lime works and salt pans, in what was a diverse industrial hub of the era.

The majority of the remains of the waggonways around Ayr are from a later era of stone blocks and iron rails. However, given the date of inception by George Taylor & Sons and Richard Oswald of Auchincruive, respectively for their parts, it is likely that the first eighteenth-century lines here were constructed from wood, in the Tyneside

The trackbed of the Auchincruive Waggonway. (Rosser1954 - Creative Commons)

style, and by 1807 the original lines had been replaced with a plateway. Whilst Robertson states that the Ayr waggonway network was abandoned by 1832, some evidence suggests that much of it remained in operation until 1872, having served Annbank Pit as late as the 1860s.

Summary

What is clear from the chronology of Scotland's early wooden railways is that for quite some time after the Cockenzie–Tranent of 1722 there was virtually nothing. There was a void in the rest of the country until at least post-1750, after which things picked up in earnest. The following six decades saw the creation of no fewer than eleven wooden railways, mainly concentrated around the coal fields of the central belt, with Brora being the outlying oddity in the far north. The rapid development in technology that these railways show between 1750 and 1811 – the laying of iron plates on top of the wooden rails; subsequent full replacement with short cast-iron rails with stone sleepers and finally through to longer malleable iron rails – shows a concerted effort to get the technology right. This collective cause of the Scottish industrialists helped drive the improvement of technology and paved the way for the age of modern railways.

CHAPTER 3

The Introduction of Iron

The introduction of iron rails was a step change in railway technology, meaning rails were more durable and could support heavier loads. Furthermore, they reduced the friction between the wheel and rail, allowing loads to be moved at a faster pace with less effort. The earliest iron railways began in England, probably at Coalbrookdale in 1767/68. They consisted of cast-iron bars 6 ft long, 3 in wide, around 1½ in thick and weighed around 70 lb per yard. They were quite crude, being cast in open moulds, and were used as 'armour plating' to existing wooden railways in order to reduce wear and extend their lifespan. Known as 'strap rails', they were secured to the uppermost rail using nails or screws.

Strap Rails

These rails appear to have been adopted quite quickly in Scotland. The first waggonway to use them was that which served the **Carron Iron Foundry**. The foundry, located just north of Falkirk, had been established in 1759 by Samuel Garbett and John Roebuck, from Birmingham, England, and William Cadell. The trio recruited several experts from Coalbrookdale and Cadell's son, William jnr, was appointed as the first manager and he had the first wooden railway built serving the foundry in 1760, bringing coal from the Kinnaird colliery 1½ miles to the north. In or by 1769, there was a further extension, 3 miles further north to Quarrole. The gauge was 3 ft 3 in, the same as at Alloa and that Cadell had used at Cockenzie. Laying the waggonway was an easy business decision to make, despite the heavy initial outlay. Before the introduction of the waggonway, carriage of materials to and from the foundry cost £1,200 a week and after it came into use the cost dropped to only £300, saving the company £10,800 per year!

During 1767 the wooden waggonway received Coalbrookdale-style wrought-iron and, soon after, cast-iron strap rails: 'Stretching from Kinnaird Colliery into the interior of the works, was constructed in 1766. The rails in that instance were of wood, covered with a sort hoop-iron. In the course of the following year, however, rails wholly of iron were cast at Colebrook Dale Iron-Works.' (Dendy Marshal 1938: 141). The 'sort of hoop-iron' suggests the use of thin wrought-iron strips, like those used by coopers to hoop barrels, nailed in

The sadly long-demolished bridge which carried the Carron Waggonway over the River Carron. It was an early iron structure, which hung off the side of the old medieval bridge. (After Dendy Marshall)

place. The cast-iron rails sourced from Coalbrookdale were very probably cast-iron strap rails; it would be very unlikely that cast-iron rails were in use at this date other than as armour plating.

The Carron Waggonway was probably obsolete by the turn of the nineteenth century as a second railway laid with cast-iron edge rails, which would become known as the 'Old Wagon Road', was built in 1810. It connected the ironworks with Bainsford Basin on the Forth & Clyde Canal. It ran most of its 2-mile length along the side of a public road. In order for the railway to cross the River Carron, a cast-iron bridge was suspended from the side of the stone road bridge which had been built in 1775. Sadly, both bridges were demolished in 1905 to make way for a new bridge.

Cast-Iron Plates and Fish-Bellies

As we have seen, the use of cast- or wrought-iron strap rails as 'armour plating' on wooden waggonways presented a technological and cost-saving advancement. The next development would be the evolution from these often quite crude cast-iron bars to rails proper. It would also see the use of iron rather than wooden wheels which further reduced the friction between wheel and rail, meaning a horse could pull an even heavier load. The earliest cast-iron rails, like those at Alloa, were simple square or rectangular section rails, often with integral feet through which they were spiked to wooden sleepers. They were crude but they worked. However, they were relatively weak and were expensive to make.

Above and below: An example of cast-iron fish-belly rails supported on stone blocks, as used on many early railways in Scotland. This example does not use chairs and is cast with integral feet which lock together like pieces of a jigsaw puzzle. (Anthony Dawson)

Extra strength could be gained by simply making them bigger or thicker, but this meant using more iron. Ideally, for a beam to have a constant strength throughout its length, its section should be increased to a maximum at its mid-span, which would entail increasing the depth of the resulting rail at its centre, the underside of the rail forming a curve or ellipse, colloquially known as a 'fish belly'. The earliest fish belly rails were cast in the late 1790s and early 1800s. Cast-iron fish-belly rails were adopted by the Tranent–Cockenzie Waggonway (see Chapter 1) in 1815. The iron rails were secured to stone sleeper blocks by cast-iron chairs, with a wooden or wrought-iron key used to create a tight fit between the rail and chair. Ballast to keep the blocks in position was usually formed from small coal, ashes and industrial waste. The Tranent–Cockenzie excavations, however, show that it was hard to keep track built like this to gauge, and that maintenance was heavy in keeping it running. There was evidence for many running and bodged repairs including inserting wooden sleepers in lieu of stone blocks, or to prop up the mid-point of the rails.

The success of Sir John Hope at Pinkie (see below) inspired his neighbours looking to solve their transport problems by building iron railways rather than wooden ones. Thus, in 1817, John Wauchope who worked the **Edmonstone Collieries** built a railway to carry coal to the nearest road – the turnpike from Edinburgh to Dalkeith. Wauchope's tacksman at Edmonstone, one Alexander Laing, agreed to build an iron railway from Newton Colliery to 'Little France' on the Edinburgh–Dalkeith road. The engineer was Robert Stevenson. The railway came into use during August 1818. An advertisement in the *Edinburgh Evening Courant* of 20 August 1818 states that 'on Monday next' the sale of 'the Best Jewel Coal' and 'Emdonstone Great Coal' would commence at 'Little France depot' which was only

A stretch of stone block railway under excavation at Cockenzie Harbour in summer 2023. The stone blocks are staggered as the track forms a curve. (Anthony Dawson)

One of the stone sleeper blocks with cast-iron chair still in situ under excavation at Cockenzie Harbour. (Anthony Dawson)

3 miles from 'the high street of Edinburgh'. The railway was nearly level throughout and used cast-iron edge rails, the wagons being capable of carrying between 8 tons 16 cwt and 11 tons, drawn by a single horse.

The other form cast-iron rails could take was the L-shaped tram plate developed by John Curr of Sheffield in the 1780s, and which was used in Scotland by the **Kilmarnock & Troon** (see Chapter 4). Unlike the earlier wooden railways where the wheels were guided by flanges on the wheels, with a plateway, the wheels were guided by a flange on the rail. The rails were mounted on stone blocks, using iron pins driven into wooden plugs in holes drilled in the blocks, a method of track-laying which became universal from around the 1790s until the late 1850s, when the first rolled steel rails were introduced.

Around 1821–23, the **Elgin Railway** used a very curious form of rail. This consisted of a cast- or wrought-iron bar rail which slotted into an inverted T-shaped chair, the rail being held in jaws in the leg of the T. These chairs were then attached to the stone blocks with bolts which passed through them, with an iron plate on the underside. Like the Alloa, the Elgin served more than just the needs of the colliery owners. At various times it carried coal to Charlestown and Limekiln harbours, and had branches to a limeworks, a foundry, brickworks and, of course, salt pans. The depot at Dunfermline was supplied by coal via the Nethertown and Pittencrief branches. The town had another depot supplied by the Venturefair Waggonway.

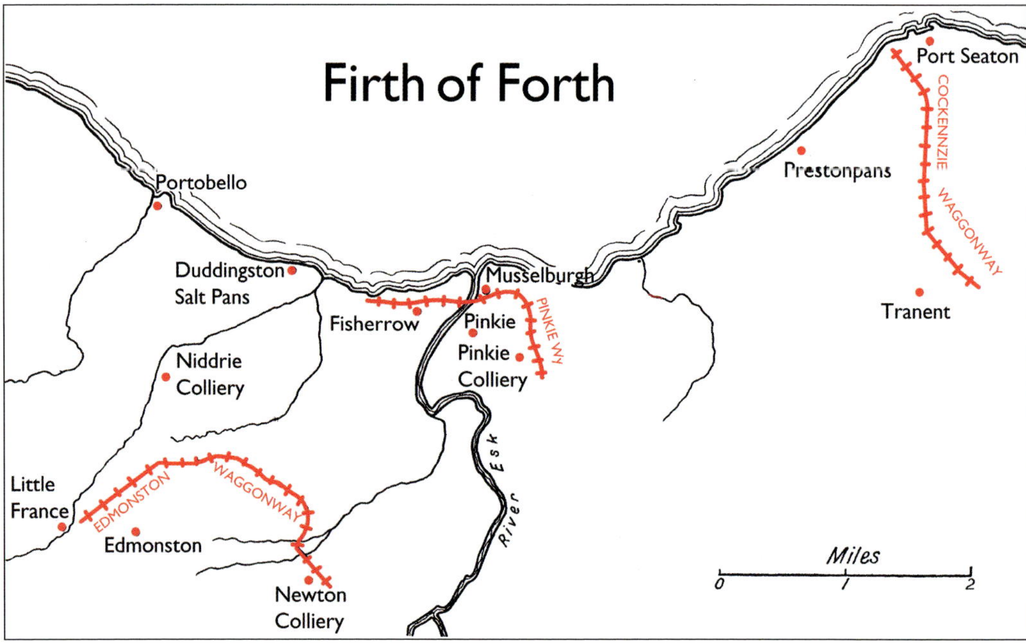

A map of the early railways of East Lothian showing the Edmonston, Pinkie, and Tranent–Cockenzie Waggonways. (Anthony Dawson)

Above and opposite above: An example of cast-iron L-shaped plate rail, carried in cast-iron chairs on stone blocks. The ends of the rails butted against each other in the chair and were secured with a single wrought-iron pin.

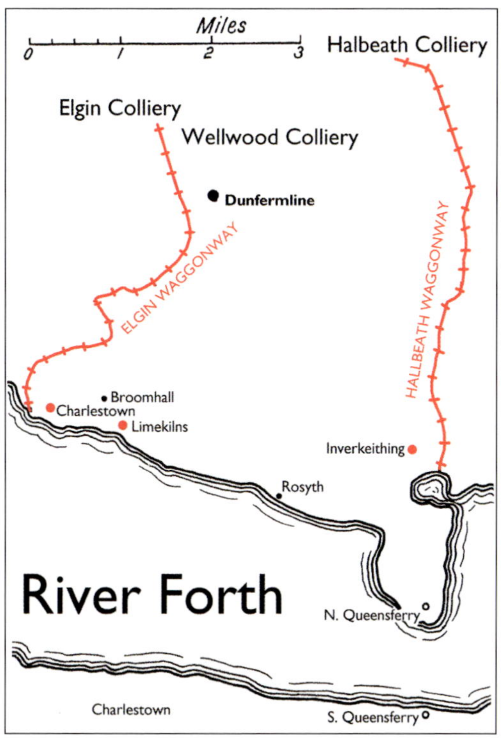

A map of Lord Elgin's Railway (alias Charlestown Railway) and the neighbouring Halbeath Railway. (Anthony Dawson)

Wrought Iron

The cost of maintaining a wooden waggonway was one of the major factors in the switch to iron. Indeed, it is possible that the first use of wrought-iron rails was in Scotland on the **Pinkie Waggonway** (see the map on p. 54). Wrought iron rail was much stronger than cast iron and could be rolled in longer sections, thus reducing the number of joints and making the ride smoother. Being slightly elastic, it could also be bent to shape and create true curves for the first time. In essence, wrought-iron rails made the locomotive-worked railway possible. Wrought-iron fish-belly rail was first rolled on a large scale by John Birkenshaw at the Bedlington Ironworks, near Morpeth, Northumberland, in 1820. However, it had been used at Tindale Fell in Cumbria on Lord Carlisle's private colliery railway sometime around 1808. Robert Stevenson became a major proponent of wrought-iron rail, and indeed George Stephenson gave him much credit for Birkenshaw's rails:

> The hints we got from your Report on Railways, which you were so kind to send me... Your reference to Tindale Fell Railway led the inventor to make some experiments on malleable iron bars, the results of which convinced him of the superiority of the malleable over the cast iron... Those rails are so much liked... and I think in a short time they will do away with the cast-iron railways.

The Pinkie Waggonway was begun by Sir John Hope (1781–1853), whose father, Sir Archibald Hope (1735–95) of Pinkie House, had 'almost a monopoly of the Edinburgh [coal] market'. His coal was of excellent quality and his pits conveniently located close

Sir John Hope, 11th Baronet of Craighall, who together with his agent John Grieve established the Pinkie Waggonway and introduced early wrought-iron rails. (National Galleries Scotland, Creative Commons 3.0)

to Edinburgh for ease of transport. However, to increase his vend and reduce transport costs, Sir John built his waggonway in 1812. The waggonway ran from his pits south-east of Musselburgh and crossed the River Esk to the harbour at Fisherrow, with an extension running a short distance west to the Pinkie salt pans. The line was constructed by Mr John Grieve. '[It] is one of the most perfect in Britain, a single horse draws five loaded waggons, each containing 30 cwt of coals, at the rate of four miles an hour – in all 7½ tons, exclusive of the waggons, which weight 3 tons more.' (Dendy Marshall 1938: 114). The waggonway was 2 miles long and Thomas Telford records that for the first third of a mile it had a falling gradient of 1 in 72; for the second third of a mile was 'nearly level' and for the final third had a rising gradient of 1 in 700. He also recorded that one horse was capable of drawing four wagons, loaded with 1½ tons of coal, and that each wagon weighed 12 cwt. One horse was able to make five trips per day.

In 1818, Robert Stevenson described how 'Experiments with Malleable Iron Rails have also been made at Mr Taylor's works at Ayr, and Sir John Hope's at Pinkie' several years before Birkenshaw rolled his first wrought-iron rail, which George Stephenson adopted on the Stockton & Darlington Railway of 1825. The possible very early use of wrought-iron rails at Pinkie is also hinted at by the *Edinburgh Encyclopaedia* (1824) which states:

> Malleable Iron was first introduced in Rail-Ways, we believe, by Mr George Grieve [*sic* John Grieve], at Sir John Hope's Collieries, near Edinburgh... The Rails consist of square bars, one inch and one and a quarter inch square, nine feet long, resting on one or two sleepers in the middle, and resting and made fast to sleepers at the extremities; a simple knee being formed on each end of the bar, and the two knees of each two adjacent Rails jammed into one socket on the sleeper.

The entry concludes: 'The use of these Rails was found so beneficial, that they have since entirely super-seded [*sic*] the Cast Iron Rail in general use at the time of their invention.'

These early rails at Pinkie were thus identical to those wrought-iron rails in use at Tindale Fell in Cumbria from around 1808. They were first used by Sir John Hope underground in the mine itself to improve haulage, then adopted above ground about ten years later. In fact, David St John Thomas states that the Pinkie Waggonway 'earned a place in history by being the first railway to use wrought-iron rails'.

The haulage of coal below ground was then carried out by children and women until 1843. One of those women, called a 'hurrier' in England or 'slype drawer' in Scotland, was Isabella Sommerville of Tranent, who in 1910 at the age of eighty-five was credited as being the 'Oldest Pit-Woman in the World'. From the age of six, she worked on her hands and knees, pulling a sled or small coal truck or 'hutch' called a 'coal slype' behind her via a chain connected to a leather belt worn around her waist, 'pulling it like a pony'. She worked at Pinkie Colliery until it closed and later learned to 'howke', or push, coal hutches and carry the coal in creels. Later, she worked at Harley Muir 'until the women were expelled in 1843' when the law banned women and children working underground.

Robert Stevenson was a major proponent of wrought-iron rails in Scotland and proposed them for all of his railway schemes. They were promoted in England by George Stephenson, who despite having taken out a patent for cast-iron fish-belly rail with William

The route of the Pinkie Waggonway as preserved near Pinkie Primary School. (Ed Bethune)

Losh in 1816, saw the immediate advantages of the new technology, causing a nasty rupture in his friendship with Losh.

Scottish railways were not far behind England in the adoption of wrought-iron rails. Wrought-iron railways were in use at Pinkie from maybe as early as 1808, certainly before Brikenshaw first rolled his patent rails. They were also used on the Monkland & Kirkintilloch and Garnkirk & Glasgow (Chapter 4) where they opened the way for the use of locomotives in Scotland. The wrought-iron rails at Pinkie:

> Certainly forms the most perfect rail which has hitherto been contrived... It is twelve feet long, two inches broad along the top, about half an inch along the bottom, and still thinner between. It rests on sleepers at every three feet, and at those places the rail is two inches deep, while in the middle point between the sleepers it is three inches deep.

The contrast between short 3-ft-long cast-iron rails and the later wrought-iron rails is visible archaeologically on the Tranent–Cockenzie Waggonway (see Chapter 1). Excavations in 2023 showed that curves laid with short cast-iron rails were not true curves, more akin to an old-fashioned 'threepenny bit' which would have increased resistance, damaged wheels and also damaged the track if vehicles passed over them at anything more than walking pace. Wrought-iron rails allowed true curves to be laid, which also meant they could be traversed at a higher speed and by locomotives. Thanks to the use of these wrought-iron rails, it was found 'by experiment' that a horse was able to 'track ten tons of goods upon a level railway, exclusively of the weight of the waggons' which was 'daily exemplified' on the Pinkie and Elgin waggonways.

The railway was worked by horsepower and incline planes, down which loaded wagons ran by gravity. Sadly, in April 1820, the 'old man' who kept the gate on the Pinkie Waggonway where it crossed a road was killed by a train of wagons: 'The loaded waggons were descending an inclined plane from the coal-pit, as usual, without assistance, when the deceased hastened to open the gate for their passage, but being unfortunately too late, he was thrown over, and five or six waggons passing over him, caused instant death.' (*Kentish Weekly Post*, 21 April 1820). A second similar accident happened a few years later when Sir John Hope's gardener, Mr Stewart, was nearly run down and killed by a train of loaded wagons. Stewart was:

> Riding a poney [*sic*] near the gate at Pinkie House, when he was met by some loaded waggons, coming down the descent on the railway, but owing to the restiveness or obstinacy of the poney, both it and the rider were thrown down by the waggons, when Mr Stewart had one of his arms so bruised and shattered, that amputation was found necessary. The poney had one of its legs broken.
>
> *Caledonian Mercury*, 13 July 1826

Quite when the Pinkie Waggonway went out of use is not clear, but in 1841 the wood and iron components, 'composing the Bridge formerly used as a Railway Bridge, and situated

The Pinkie Waggonway ran past this entrance lodge to the grounds of Pinkie Castle. It's easy to see why there were so many accidents given how close the waggonway ran to people's homes and down the street of Musselburgh. (Ed Bethune)

The site of the iron bridge which carried the Pinkie Waggonway over the River Esk. The patch of brickwork in the retaining wall probably marks where the bridge stood. (Ed Bethune)

at the North extremity of the River Esk', were offered for sale, but the sale was postponed before it could take place.

Whilst strap rails, and later cast-iron rails, were sufficient for the loads pulled by horse, if Scotland's railways were to develop further and see the introduction of locomotive power a new track system was required: wrought iron. As we shall see in the next chapter, Scottish engineers were no less advanced or adventurous in adopting steam than their English counterparts.

Summary

Development of railway technology in Scotland mirrored that in England, and in many instances Scottish coal owners were not far behind their English cousins in adopting new technologies: strap rails were in use in Scotland twelve to eighteen months after their apparent first adoption at Coalbrookdale. Equally, cast- and later wrought-iron rails were adopted pretty much simultaneously on both sides of the border, demonstrating a flourishing interchange of ideas and technology. By the 1820s, Scottish railways were no less technologically advanced than their English counterparts.

Chapter 4

The Coming of Steam

The Kilmarnock & Troon Railway (1812)

Whilst Scotland had been a relative latecomer to railways, it was not necessarily so when it came to locomotives. The Kilmarnock & Troon Railway was perhaps the first 'railway' in Scotland in a legal sense: it was the first railway in Scotland to be authorised by an Act of Parliament; it had capital held in publicly traded shares; and, unlike the waggonways before it, was authorised to be worked mechanically but not to carry passengers, although this did not stop it from being the first passenger railway in Scotland. The only part of the K&TR which was not 'modern', however, was its track, which used cast-iron L-shaped tram plates rather than edge rails.

The K&TR was envisaged to carry coal from Ayrshire pits near Kilmarnock down to the coastal town of Troon for onward shipping by sea. Thanks to the K&TR, Scottish railways were no longer the private property of a coal owner (or coal owners) and generally working over a short distance. However, like the earlier waggonways, they had been built to solve the same problem: the cost of transporting coal from pits to the nearest port. Much of the output of Ayrshire's pits went to Ireland, and the cost of carting coal could

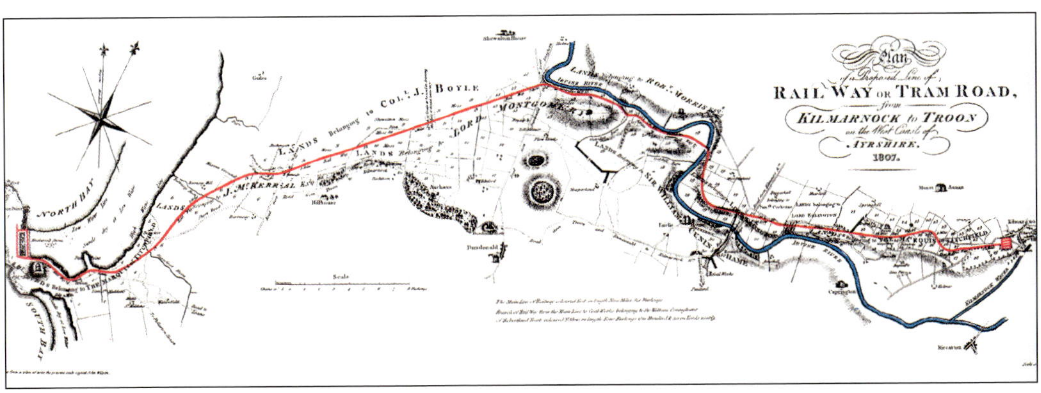

A contemporary map of the Kilmarnock & Troon Railway showing its route from Coal Pits, near Kilmarnock, to the coast at Troon and the new harbour for onward coastal shipping.

be prohibitively expensive, even over relatively short distances. Despite the expense, something like 8,000 tons of Ayrshire coal, or around 40 pr cent of total production, was still carried by carts to the sea at Irvine as it headed to Ireland. To obviate the cost of road transport, in 1806, a canal was proposed and William Henry Cavendish Bentinck, the Marquis of Titchfield – from 1809 the 4th Duke of Portland – and the largest landowner in Ayrshire, proposed to develop a harbour at Troon. Instead of the expensive canal, however, in 1808, Titchfield suggested the construction of a railway which would be much cheaper to construct and in terms of land required to be purchased. An Act of Parliament was obtained on 27 May 1808.

To build the railway, Titchfield needed to raise capital and do so quickly. He appointed William Jessop as his engineer. Jessop quoted £38,167 10*s*. 0*d*. to build and equip the railway and eighty shares of £500 each were made available. To attract prospective investors, it was advertised that the line would return some 20 per cent on its initial investment. Unfortunately, Titchfield was unable to encourage many of his neighbouring landowners to invest in the project and ultimately had to purchase sixty-seven shares himself. His daughter, Lady Margaret Bentinck, acquired ten; Lord Montgomerie one share; the Earl of Eglington one share; and Colonel John Boyle of Shewalton one share. The total raised through the sale of shares was £38,500, which would cover the cost of construction plus a little surplus for contingencies. Titchfield also invested a further £60,000 building a harbour at Troon, the total cost of the project coming in at around £100,000.

Jessop, who had been the engineer of the Surrey Iron Railway, was no stranger to Scotland as he had worked with Thomas Telford on the Caledonian Canal. Engineering, other than crossing Shoalton Moss and construction of the Laigh Milton Viaduct at Gatehead, was relatively straightforward. The viaduct is Scotland's oldest railway viaduct; it was Scotland's first railway viaduct to carry a locomotive and is probably the earliest surviving viaduct from a public railway. It is built of four arches, each with a 40-ft span, carrying the railway 26 ft above the River Irvine. It was closed in 1846 when the line was re-engineered to avoid curves which proved too sharp for locomotive operation.

In January 1812, the *Scots Magazine* carried a lengthy description of the line and its construction, noting that Troon would boast 'one of the best harbours in Ayrshire' and that the railway would be 'of great advantage forming communication' between Kilmarnock and Troon. It was a 'very great work of improvement' carried out by the by now Duke of Portland not only for Ayrshire but Scotland in general. Jessop engineered the line on a falling gradient favouring loaded wagons heading to the harbour. The total rise was 80 or 84 ft from Troon to Kilmarnock, the railway having 'a declivity of nearly eight feet, every mile, which is less than one sixteenth of an inch every yard'.

The track was cast-iron L-shaped tram plates, 3 ft long and weighing 40 lb each. The tread was 4-in wide and the upstanding flange was 4-in tall. Underneath the rail was a rib, 4-in thick at the middle of the rail, but tapering at each end. The ends of the rails formed feet, 'somewhat broader at both ends of each rail, to make them lie more solid on the blocks'. Sleepers were blocks of stone, 12 in sq and 9- or 10-in thick. The ends of each rail locked together and formed a single concave hole through which a broad-headed wrought-iron spike passed into a 6-in-long oak plug set into a hole drilled in the centre of each block.

The gauge was 4 ft feet over the flanges and the railway was double track with an Up and Down line as well as numerous passing places 'and with frequent communications from

The magnificent Laigh Milton Viaduct was built to carry the Kilmarnock & Troon over the River Irving in 1811. It is a magnificent monument to the pioneering days of railways. (Rosser45 via Creative Commons)

The K&T was laid using cast-iron L-shaped plates mounted on stone sleepers like these, photographed at Bugsworth Basin in Derbyshire. (Anthony Dawson)

the one road to the other so as not only to admit of carriages going both ways, but to allow one carriages to pass another when travelling in the same direction'.

What would now be termed the 'six foot' between the rails was 4 ft. Ballast was made from broken stone, topped with sand and crushed stone to form a solid road surface for the horses which pulled the wagons to walk on. The ballast was sufficiently deep to cover the stone blocks and most of the rails, 'near to the top of the ledges [*sic* flanges] of the rails'. The majority of the rails for constructing the line were made by the Glenbuck Iron Company. By 1813 the company had been paid £13,345 for about 72,000 rails; this was about a third of the entire engineering cost of building the line.

Despite the higher friction between wheel and rail of plate rails compared with edge rails, the K&TR still had an advantage over road transport: 8¾*d.* to 1*s.* 5*d.* per ton by road but only 3½*d.* by rail, and at a quicker rate. It was estimated a single horse would be able to pull a load of 10 to 12 tons descending to Troon but only 8 or 10 'in the contrary direction'. At Troon Harbour, the duke was busy constructing a new pier, 500-ft long, 30-ft high and varying in width from 65 to 30 ft against which ships could be moored to be loaded with coal. The harbour was completed in 1819 at a final cost of £200,000. The new harbour was so constructed that 'even at ebb will admit vessels of very considerable size'. It was estimated that at low tide there would be a minimum of 10 ft of water in the harbour.

Waggons on the K&T would have been similar to this replica seen at Bugsworth Basin. As the flange is on the rail, it means the wheels are smooth and any vehicle, as long as it was of the appropriate gauge, could be run on it. (Anthony Dawson)

The railway began operation on 6 July 1812 at a final cost of £59,849, or £6,300 per mile, costing more than half again of the original estimate (a 52 per cent overspend). It was operated as a railed turnpike so that any user was able to do so upon payment of a fixed toll and so long as their vehicle was of the appropriate gauge: the use of plate rails meant that any road cart could be used, whereas if edge rails had been adopted, vehicles with flanged wheels would be useable. This was noted by the American observer William Strickland, who visited in 1826, and commented that 'besides the rail waggons, common carts are introduced upon the rails' but that this had a 'very injurious effect, arising from the roughness of the tire of their wheels, and from the soil which adheres to them being deposited on the flat part of the rails'.

The company paid its first dividend in 1817, although at 5 per cent this was much less than the advertised 20 per cent. However, the K&TR would do well over the next few years handling coal.

As it was open to all users, it was the first railway in Scotland to officially carry passengers, these being carried by waggon as early as August 1811. This is attested to by a fatal accident which killed one traveller and injured several more:

> A melancholy accident happened six miles from Kilmarnock on Saturday last; [24 August 1811] the waggon was returning with a number of people from the Troon by the railway when harnessing gave way and owing to the darkness of the night, the waggon tumbled down a precipice of seven or eight feet perpendicular. One man unfortunately was killed and some so severely hurt that their lives are despaired of.
>
> *The Glasgow Herald*, 30 August 1811

In 1819, the engineer Robert Stevenson noted 'the conveyance of passengers, has not been attempted, excepting perhaps, from Kilmarnock to Troon', the service being operated, perhaps erratically, by William Paterson of Kilmarnock. The driver was William 'Willie' Wright, a local man. The local newspaper, the *Advertiser Times Herald* of 15 June 1812, announced that William Paterson would begin carrying passengers travelling from Kilmarnock to Troon 'upon the Iron Railway' from Saturday 27 June, from Gargieston, 'until the road is forwarded to Kilmarnock', i.e. the line was not completed, 'and every Tuesday, Thursday and Saturday, afterwards at quarter past nine in the morning; and will leave Troon at six o'clock the same evening'. Tickets would cost 1*s.* and goods would be handled from Kilmarnock to Gargieston by a local road carrier. Paterson would 'also accommodate any Family (who find it inconvenient on the aforesaid days) on any other day of the week'. This service was obviously seasonal, during summer months, as Paterson advertised the following spring (1813) that it would recommence, with the 'inside fare' costing 2*s.* 6*d.* and 1*s.* 6*d.* or 1*s.* for 'outside' passengers who sat on the roof. A single fare was 1*s.* 6*d.* The journey time was estimated at two hours. One feature of the journey was a stop at Drybridge, where both men and horses were refreshed at an inn close to the railway.

In 1818, the French engineer Charles Dupin visited the K&TR and observed that: 'I have seen diligences established on the iron railway from Kilmarnock to Troon Bay, they give the idea of an enormous nomad's caravan, and yet are drawn without any effort by a single horse.' (*The Scots Magazine*, 1 November 1818). The names of two, perhaps three, vehicles are known: a fully enclosed stagecoach-type vehicle named the *Caledonia* and an open carriage called *The Boat*; a third, the *Fair Trader*, is also recorded. According to the company minutes, in 1830, a Mrs Jean Brown of Troon was given permission to run a 'jaunting car' on the line. At the same time, Willie Wight was allowed to run an additional vehicle. During the late 1830s the K&TR was carrying 20,000 passengers per year, representing two or three return trips per day, increasing to four or five return trips during the summer.

Although the K&TR was designed to be worked by horses, this did not stop the Duke of Portland from trying to adopt the latest technology from England. The use of locomotives was known about in Scotland, the *Caledonian Mercury* in September 1811 reporting favourably on the experiments by Blenkinsop & Murray at the Middleton Railway, Leeds, and that horses were soon to be 'discarded'. The locomotives on the Middleton Railway were the first steam locomotives in commercial operation, and the first to be built in any number, coming into use in summer 1812.

Thus, in October 1813, Portland's agent, John Bailey, entered into correspondence with John Watson, of the Kenton & Coxlodge Railway, near Newcastle upon Tyne, where a pair of Blenkinsop & Murray rack locomotives were at work. Bailey enquired as to the cost of locomotive working and advantages which could be gained from it. Watson informed him that a locomotive would cost £380 and that they were capable of moving a load of 64 tons gross on the level and that the initial outlay would be recouped by laying off men and horses. However, because of the weight of Blenkinsop's locomotive, and that they used a specialist type of track which had the rack cast as part

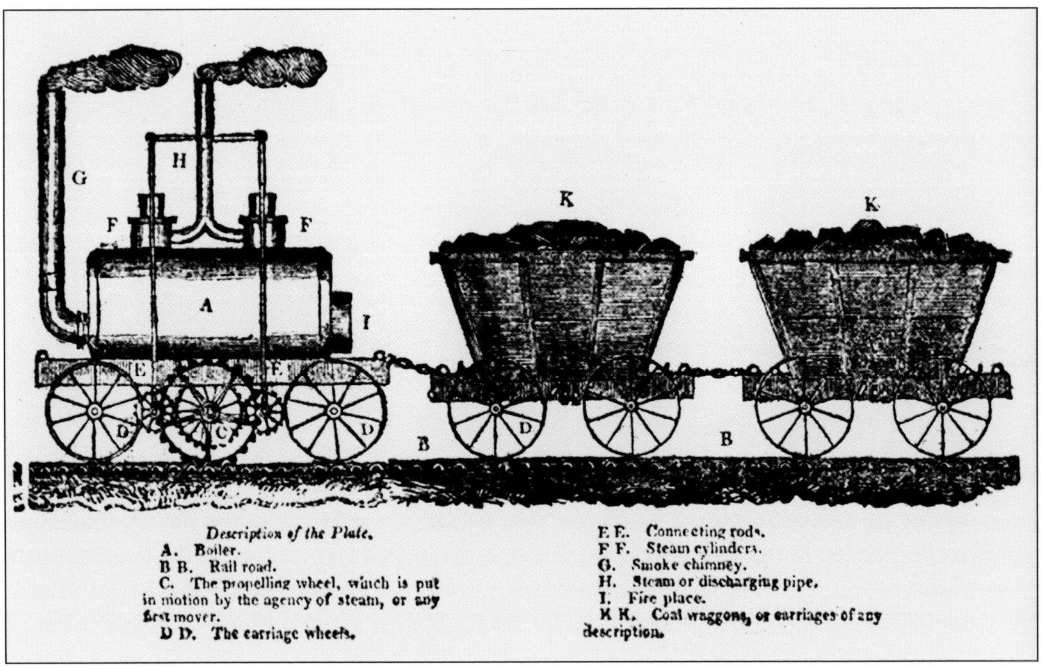

A contemporary depiction of John Blenkinsop's patent rack locomotive, first used on the Middleton Railway in Leeds. It was the first commercially successful steam locomotive in the world. It was a locomotive like this which was proposed to run on the K&T. (Anthony Dawson)

A replica of a Blenkinsop & Murray rack wheel on display at the Middleton Railway in Leeds. It was cast in 2012 to mark the bicentenary of steam railways. (Anthony Dawson)

An original section of toothed cast-iron rail which engaged with the large rack wheel which pulled the locomotive along, seen here at the Middleton Railway in Leeds. It was because of the cost of completely relaying the K&T with new patent rail that locomotive working was put on hold. (Anthony Dawson)

of the rail, it would mean relaying the entire railway at a cost of £352 per mile. So, this was clearly a non-starter.

Locomotive working lay in abeyance for only a few years. In 1816, the Duke of Portland attempted steam locomotion again, but this time using a purely adhesion-worked locomotive, an 0-6-0 purchased from George Stephenson. George Stephenson was the premier locomotive and railway engineer of his day. In 1815 and 1816, he had taken out patents for steam locomotives, wheels and rails. His 1816 patent included a six-wheel locomotive fitted with 'steam springs' to lessen the shock of the mass of the locomotive over the brittle cast-iron rails then in use, with the wheels being coupled by a chain. In the event, even the use of springs and six wheels to spread the weight of the engine over the rails would not be sufficient. Furthermore, unlike Stephenson's standard locomotives which had flanged wheels running on an edge rail, the K&TR locomotive had smooth wheels to run on a plateway. This meant that the friction between the iron driving wheels and the upstanding flange of the rails was considerable.

A local man, the artist John Kelso Hunter, observed the engine when it started at Kilmarnock, and many years later recalled what he had seen as a boy:

> The carcase sat on three pairs of wheels. The fore and aft pair were turned by long connecting rods fixed to a knob on the outer flange of the wheels and by the aid of cross-beams played up and down like a pair of frame-saws, turning the wheels like so many grindstones. On the centre of each axle-tree was a wheel with teeth, and an open chain revolved on the teeth in pinion form, keeping the valves in their place... The locomotive was, like some great folk, before its time, as they had not yet discovered a way for its will. The road that used to be trod by the auld horse was in some places high in the centre, and on those heights did the teeth wheels on the axle trees rest, bending both them and the rods by which motion was attained. As a power out of place, the giant had to be laid aside for a time.

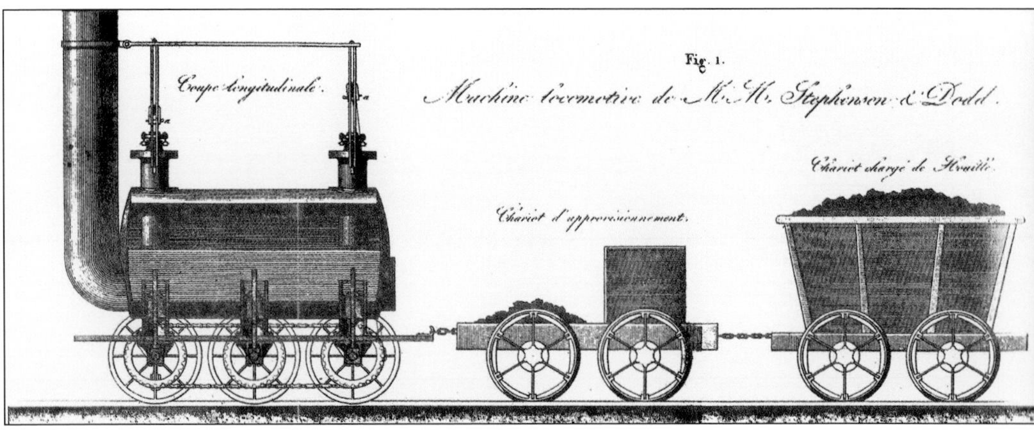

A side view and cross section of George Stephenson's patent 1816 locomotive, carried on six wheels and with a chain to couple the driven axles so as to synchronise the cylinders. *The Duke* for the K&TR was built to this design. (Anthony Dawson)

Hunter notes that many of the locals were terrified and in awe of the new machine:

> The engineer opened the safety-valve with a grand burst, which struck the air and the ears of the crowd at the same moment. It seemed to me as if the whole mass had been blown to fragments. The crowd instinctively swelled to such a size as burst the boundaries of the hedges on both sides... All sorts of murder shouts arose from the group. I was petrified, and held a death grip for a time, quite uncertain whether the people were killed, or if I were still alive.

The locomotive was able to draw 10 tons – so no more than a horse could – but at twice the speed, around 5 miles an hour. However, as George Buchanan recalled, although the locomotive worked well, it was too heavy for the rails, despite him estimating that it only weighed 5 tons. Indeed, examination of K&TR records demonstrate a rapid rise in the breakage of plate rails from September 1816 which could be attributed to damage by a locomotive. They also show continued breakages and experimentation with different patterns of rail and larger stone sleepers. By 1819 new heavier rails of a more refined designed had been introduced. Even with these heavier rails, locomotive working was apparently given up but perhaps only after a protracted struggle. Or maybe not: in 1821 a local farmer complained about 'Cinders from a Steam Engine Waggon going along the Railway' which had set fire to his crops.

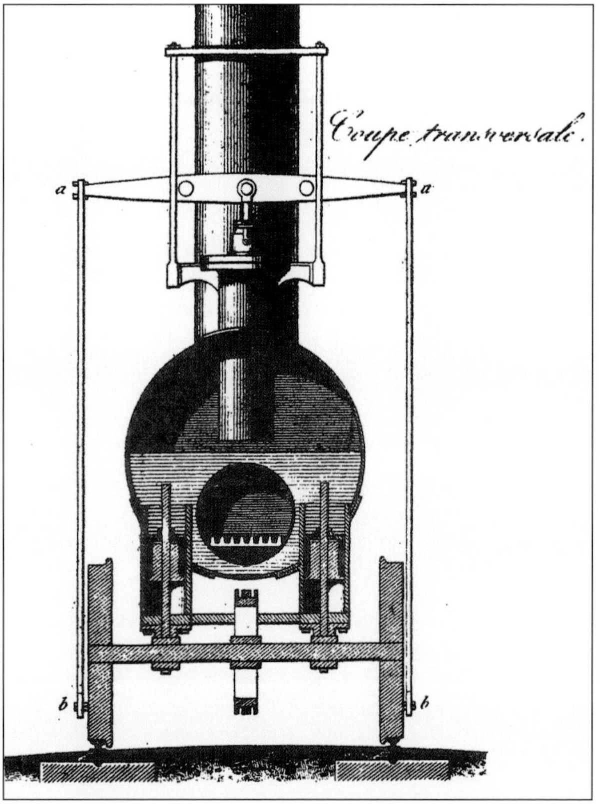

An end view and cross section of the Stephenson 1816 locomotive showing the large-diameter fire tube; vertical cylinders and 'steam springs' which provided an early, crude, form of suspension. (Anthony Dawson)

Thus, after this initial flirtation with steam, the K&TR would be a horse-drawn railway until 1841 when its successor, the Glasgow, Paisley, Kilmarnock & Ayr Railway, re-laid it with wrought-iron edge rails. However, there is a persistent myth that the Stephenson locomotive – or perhaps another one – fitted with lighter wooden wheels, ran on the line until 1848. Samuel Smiles notes that the locomotive had cost £750 but when it was sold for scrap only realised £13. There is a suggestion that the locomotive was sold to the 7th Earl of Elgin for use on his railway in Fife in October 1824 at a cost of £70. Once again, it was found too heavy for the cast-iron rails, and instead it was used as a stationary pumping engine at Lord Elgin's limestone quarry in 1825. In 1830, it was transferred to one of Elgin's collieries near Dunfermline and its fate thereafter is unknown.

In 1846, the K&TR was leased to its bigger neighbour, the Glasgow, Paisley, Kilmarnock & Ayr Railway. The K&TR Company continued to exist, however, receiving the lease charges, until 16 July 1899 when the line was bought by the GP&K's successor, the Glasgow & South Western Railway. The K&TR was finally wound up in 1902.

Charles Maclaren – 'Father of the Railways'

Charles Maclaren (1782–1866) was the founder and editor of the influential *The Scotsman* newspaper. He was a fellow of the Royal Society of Edinburgh, fellow of the Geological Society and President of the Edinburgh Geological Society. He was an early and eager advocate of railways. During 1824, on the front of four consecutive issues of *The Scotsman*, he published a dissertation promoting a railway system. He counselled that railways should be much more than feeders to canals or coal carriers. He saw them as a joined-up network, powered by steam locomotives. He wrote:

> We are quite satisfied that the introduction of the locomotive steam power has given a decided superiority to railways. Indeed, we are convinced, and we hope... that the general use of railways and steam carriages for all kinds of internal communication opens up prospects of almost boundless improvement and is destined perhaps to work a greater change in the state of civil society...

His essay was published in England and the United States in 1825. It was also translated into French and German and soon after the Edinburgh Association for Railway Experiments was formed. The *Glasgow Herald* opined in November 1824 that the locomotive was 'nearly perfect in construction' and that one engine in charge of a man and boy could do the work of ten canal boats, ten horses and twenty men. Everything seemed to be set for a second Scottish revolution.

Monkland & Kirkintilloch (1826)

The Monkland & Kirkintilloch Railway was the first railway in Scotland to use wrought-iron rails on a large scale. It also boasted the first Scottish-built locomotive, albeit a modification of an English Stephenson design.

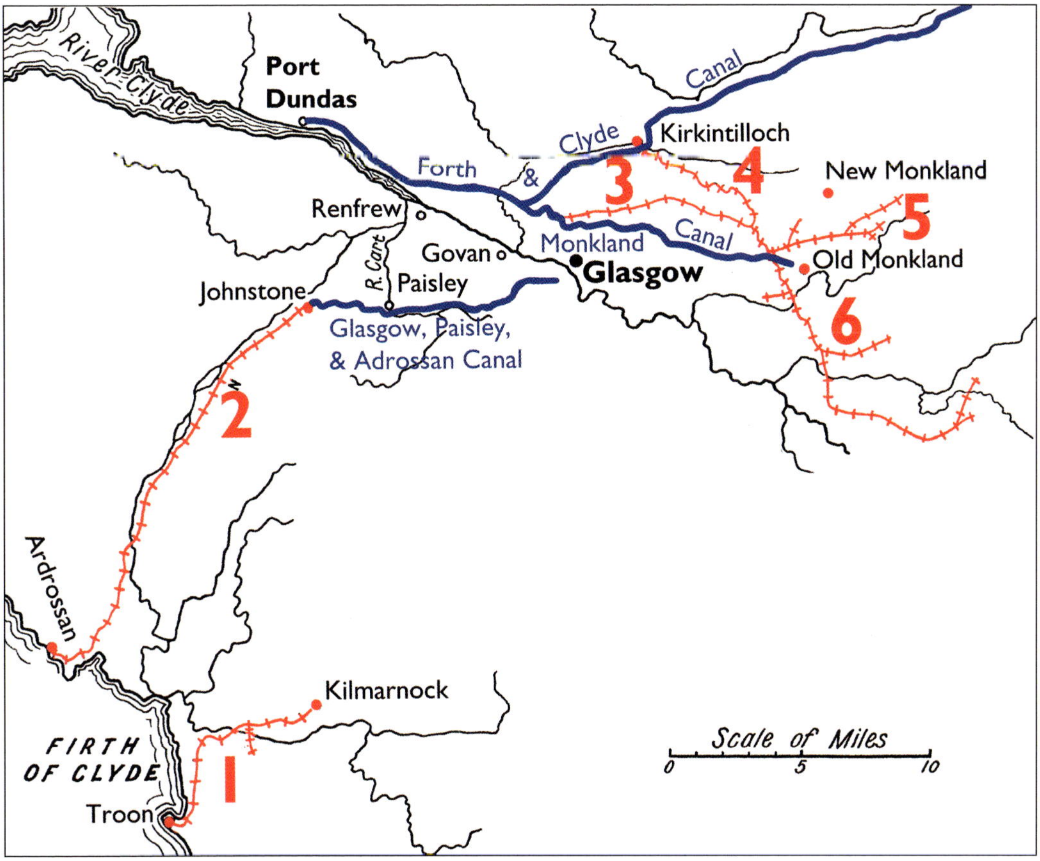

A map of the early railways in the Glasgow area: 1. Kilmarnock & Troon (1812); 2. Johnstone & Ardrossan (1831); 3. Garnkirk & Glasgow (1831); 4. Monkland & Kirkintilloch (1826); 5. Ballochney (1827); 6. Wishaw & Coltness (1833). (Anthony Dawson)

Like the other railways which had come before, the *raison d'être* of the M&KR was to move coal, in this instance to the burgeoning city of Glasgow for domestic and industrial use. The railway would link the coal pits and iron works to the Forth and Clyde Canal at Kirkintilloch, thereby escaping the monopoly of the Monkland Canal of 1794. It also opened the possibility of selling coal in Edinburgh. An Act of Parliament was granted on 17 May 1824. Share capital was £32,000 and the company had powers to raise a further £10,000 by additional shares or borrowing.

Thomas Grainger was the engineer and it was his first railway commission. Adverts inviting estimates from 'Road Engineers' for the 'forming of the Monkland and Kirkintilloch Railway' appeared in the local press in July and December 1824. The *Perthshire Courier* hoped that the railway would be a great success and would lower the cost of house coal to 1*s.* 6*d.* per ton from the existing rate of 4*s.* per ton by the canal.

Construction proceeded quickly, with track laying beginning in summer 1825. However, judging by adverts in the English newspapers for Northumberland and County Durham, Grainger and his assistant, John Miller, who were road engineers by trade, had no experience of laying railway track. One advertisement dated 4 June 1825 appeared in the *Durham County Advertiser*:

> Wanted Immediately. A person, who has considerable experience, and thoroughly understands the most improved method of laying Rail-road Bars, practised in the neighbourhood of Newcastle to act as FOREMAN in laying rails on the Monkland and Kirkintilloch Rail-way. The rails to be laid are of malleable iron, made under Mr Birkenshaw's Patent.
>
> *Durham County Advertiser*, 11 June 1825

Grainger and Miller settled on a gauge of 4 ft 6 in, as used by the other colliery lines in the area but also given their involvement in many other Scottish railway schemes, 4 ft 6 in having become the almost unofficial Scottish 'standard gauge'. In October 1825, it was reported that the railway was nearing completion, having cost around £32,000 for the 11 miles, and that it would be open in spring 1826.

The railway opened in May 1826, the *Glasgow Herald* on Friday 19 May 1826 announcing that: 'The Monkland and Kirkintilloch Railway has been opened. Wednesday one horse dragged 16 tons of coals from Cargill Colliery, Mr Colt's to Kirkintilloch. The work was accomplished in two hours with ease.' However, this may not have marked the beginning of the railway as the *Caledonian Mercury* of 29 May 1826 notes that this was probably part of a series of trial runs superintended by Grainger. He found that a single horse could pull a train of eight 18-cwt waggons, each carrying a load of 42 cwt net, the gross load being 24 tons. With this 'prodigious load' one horse led this train the 6½ miles from Gartsherry Colliery to the depot at Kirkintilloch in one hour fifty-two minutes, the total journey time in fact being two hours as, according to the *Caledonian Mercury*, 'owing to some mistake, one of the guides which direct the waggons into the passing places, was turned the wrong way, and by this oversight the train was stopped fully eight minutes'. The use of wrought-iron edge rails was seen as a huge leap forward in railway technology: the rails were longer than the old cast-iron rails, much stronger and, unlike the plate rails used by the likes of the K&TR, had lower friction. The *Caledonian Mercury* estimated that the use of wrought-iron edge rails meant a huge saving in horses, and that given the state of the roads at that time to move a comparable load 'along the common road... would have required 24 horses'. Furthermore, they could only have made one trip in a day, whilst via the railway they could make two trips per day, five days a week, saving an estimated forty horses which would have been required to do the same amount of work. The line opened to the public in October the same year.

Grainger was fully aware of railway developments south of border: first with the opening of the Stockton & Darlington Railway in 1825, which was worked by a combination of stationary engines, locomotives and horses, and the Liverpool & Manchester Railway of 1830, which was worked entirely by locomotives and conclusively proved the superiority of the locomotive over other forms of motive power. Furthermore, the neighbouring Garnkirk & Glasgow Railway had announced it would be opening with steam locomotives. Thus, the M&KR ordered its first locomotive from Murdoch, Aitken and Company of Glasgow. It was delivered on 10 May 1831. It was essentially a copy of the Stephenson Killingworth-type locomotive developed fifteen years before and which had been trialled

Above: At the spot where the Monkland & Kirkintilloch Railway once crossed Glenboig Main Street there are some old stone sleepers built into a roadside wall. The holes are where the chairs that held the rails were fixed with iron pins. (North Lanarkshire Museums)

Right: An example of one of the iron pins used to secure the chairs to the stone blocks. (North Lanarkshire Museums)

on the K&TR; a second locomotive of the same type was delivered in September 1831. They were designed by George Dodds, engineer to the K&TR, who was assisted by his son, William. The locomotives were designed to be able to move a load of 60 tons gross at 5 mph.

They were remarkably archaic machines for their date. They had two vertical cylinders (10½ in x 24 in) set on the centre line of the boiler and partially immersed in it. The boiler was 9-ft long, 4-ft 6-in diameter, but whereas Stephenson's Killingworth originals had a single large-diameter flue passing through the boiler, instead sixty 1.5-in outside diameter

A contemporary illustration of one of the Dodds locomotives as used on the Monkland & Kirkintolloch. Its origins in Stephenson's Killingworth type are obvious, albeit it is fitted with a multi-tubular boiler and internal firebox. (Anthony Dawson)

copper tubes were used instead. The four wooden wheels were 4-ft diameter. Their long chimneys, however, precluded their use through the Chrystown Tunnel, which meant that one locomotive worked the line either side of the tunnel, with the tunnel section still being worked by horses! The tunnel was opened out at a cost of £750 as part of the doubling of the line in 1832. So successful was the design that two more were built for the M&KR, and three similar locomotives for the Wishaw & Coltness Railway in 1840.

The Scotsman published an account of the first trip made by the No. 1 locomotive of the M&KR in its edition of 14 May 1831:

> On Tuesday, 10 May, he was gratified by a ride on a locomotive engine on the Monkland and Kirkintilloch Railway… It was taken from the workshop, Hill Street, on Tuesday Morning and being started on the railway below Chrystown, it passed several miles along the railway, sometimes going at the rate of fifteen miles an hour – although the company's engines are not required to move when loaded at a greater speed than 4 miles an hour.

It is recorded that these locomotives worked effectively and efficiently for four years, 'without losing a trip'. One of the problems William Dodds faced was finding and training suitable locomotive crews. There were no serious accidents involving them, other than one incident reminiscent of the Ealing Comedy *The Titfield Thunderbolt* when one of the locomotives, due to an obstruction on the rails at a level crossing, left the track and continued to run along a turnpike road! Sadly, George Dodds was killed in an accident on the railway in January 1835 and William was appointed as his successor. William would resign in 1845 and went to work for the Liverpool & Manchester Railway in England. Not only did the M&KR break new ground in Scottish railway history by using the first locomotives built in Scotland, it was also the first railway to build its own locomotives, No. 3 and No. 4, at its works at Greenside, with William Dodds being credited with the construction of No. 3. It entered service in spring 1834 and had slightly smaller cylinders than the first pair, only 10⅜-in diameter. Weight in working order was 13 tons 12¾ cwt. Locomotive No. 4 was begun in 1835 but was not completed until June 1838, the work, going by payments made toward the cost of building, taking place in phases during that period. Despite the presence of these four locomotives, the line was still also worked by horses until 1847, and all company-owned horses were sold the following year.

A passenger service on the M&KR began in 1828. *The Scotsman* reported that:

> **Railway Coach.** The first railway coach constructed in Scotland for the conveyance of passengers, made a trial journey in the neighbourhood of Airdrie on Tuesday. It is dragged by one horse, and is to ply on the Kirkintilloch Railway, in carrying passengers to boats on the canal. It is meant to carry 24 passengers, but started in high style with no less than forty, within and without.
>
> *The Scotsman*, 12 July 1828

Although clearly the K&TR passenger service predated it by a decade, as with the K&TR it demonstrated that this was no mere coal railway. The opening of the Garnkirk & Glasgow

A large-scale model of one of the M&K locomotives on display in Edinburgh. (Anthony Dawson)

Railway showed how quickly the M&KR was left behind in the rapid development of railway technology. The latter was using fast, modern Planet and Samson-type locomotives running at speeds and pulling loads unachievable by the antiquated Dodds locomotives. Furthermore, because of its narrow gauge it was also being left behind particularly with the opening of the Edinburgh–Glasgow mainline in 1844 to 4-ft 8½-in gauge. The M&KR and G&GR both regauged in 1847. A year later, it became a core constituent of the Monkland Railways, which would be absorbed by the Edinburgh & Glasgow Railway in 1865.

The Dundee & Newtyle Railway (1826)

The Dundee & Newtyle Railway was the first railway in the north of Scotland and was built to carry goods from Strathmore down to the port at Dundee. It was, despite the optimism of its promoters, far from being a success.

It began life in 1825 when Dundee Burgh Council decided to fund a survey for a railway, which would have been far cheaper than a canal scheme proposed a few years earlier in 1817. Charles Landale undertook the survey, and his route required several rope-worked inclined planes to raise the line to its summit, 532 ft above sea level. There

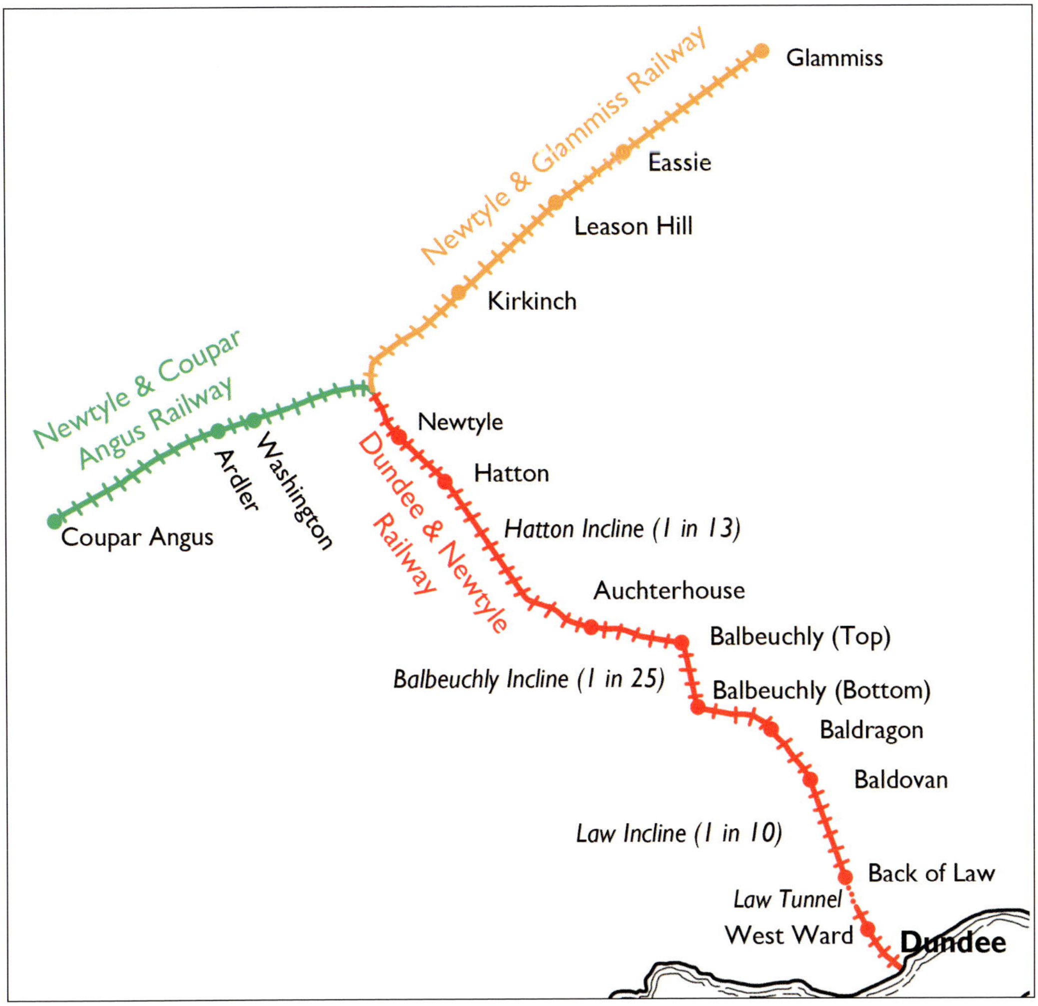

A map of the Dundee & Newtyle Railway showing its later extensions to Coupar Angus and Glammiss. (Anthony Dawson)

were three inclines in total. The first, the Law Incline, 1,060-yd (970 m) long, climbed at 1 in 10 immediately from the Dundee terminal. This was followed by the 330-yd (300 m) Law Tunnel. Next came a level section, 4¾ miles long, and then a second climb, this time for 1,700 yd (1,600 m) at 1 in 25 up the Balbeuchly Incline. A second level section of 4¾ miles preceded the third incline (the Hatton Incline), down which the line descended for 1,000 yd (910 m) at 1 in 13 to Newtyle. There was no community at Newtyle at that time from where workforce or traffic could commence. Moreover, the terminus on Ward Road, Dundee, was not close to the harbour or even the waterfront! Yet, despite these problems, the railway received its Enabling Act on 26 May 1826. Authorised capital was £30,000 in 600 £50 shares and the company was authorised to raise a further £10,000 through loans or sales of shares.

The estimated cost of the railway was some £25,600 including £3,700 for the supply of the three stationary steam engines to work the incline planes, but excluded the cost of land acquisition which would add to the problems encountered by the promoters when local landowners charged far more for their land than had been anticipated. The line was built to the peculiar gauge of 4 ft 6½ in and used fish-belly rails laid on stone blocks.

It opened in stages between 1831 and 1832, major problems being encountered with the excavation of the Law Tunnel which was completed after Herculean efforts in January which had robbed other sections of the line of labour, so that work had effectively ground to a standstill. Suffice to say, Landale was dismissed amid numerous complaints that he failed to control the contractors properly, and that he had considerably overspent.

At first horses were used on the two level stretches of line, but in 1833 steam traction was introduced. Two Planet-type 2-2-0 locomotives (Nos 32 and 33) were ordered on 15 August 1832 from Robert Stephenson & Co. to take the place of horses on the level sections, but these were subsequently cancelled. Instead, two locomotives of local construction by C. & J. Carmichael of Dundee were ordered. They were a pair of unusual 0-2-4 bogey engines named the *Earl of Airlie* and *Lord Wharncliffe,* delivered in autumn 1833. A third bogey locomotive, the *Trotter,* was delivered by Stirling & Co. the following year. They had multi-tubular Stephenson-type boilers and fireboxes but vertical cylinders – one on each side of the boiler – driving the leading wheels via bell cranks. A four-wheel bogey

The right-hand-side view of the *Earl of Airlie* as preserved and 'restored' in the 1860s. The boiler was probably originally lagged with wooden cladding. The vertical cylinders and piston valves, together with the bell-crank drive, are very apparent. (Anthony Dawson)

Another 1860s photograph of the *Earl of Airlie*. The external regulator and steam pipes are obvious, so too the small dome over the firebox on which the two safety valves are mounted. (Anthony Dawson)

supported the firebox end. The trio of locally built locomotives must have worked well enough, but a Stephenson Samson class locomotive – which according to Whishaw was named *John Bull* – was supplied in April 1836 (order 137) at a cost, including the tender, of £1,137. *John Bull* began operation on 26 May but broke her crank axle in July with a replacement being sent from Newcastle.

The D&NR can never be said to have been prosperous. In 1834, plans were prepared to extend the line from its existing terminus in Ward Road to the harbour side. At the same time, the Burgh Council wanted to improve its harbour facilities and the extension of the railway complemented this. The line was laid along Lindsay Street, then ran across Nethegate to Yeaman Shore, before turning east to join Dundee Harbour's own internal railway lines. There was to be a steep incline of 1 in 24 to reach the harbour and horses were only able to move two loaded wagons at a time. A new Act received Royal Assent in 1836 which allowed the raising of a further £100,000 through the sale of 2,000 £50 shares, but most of them were allocated to creditors as investors were unwilling to buy shares in the concern. The extension was completed in February 1837.

Two branches were built: the Newtyle & Couper Angus Railway was authorised on 21 July 1835 and the Newtyle & Glammiss Railway ten days later. A new joint line from

Newtyle was built, which then diverged to the south-west toward Coupar and the north-east toward Glammiss (nowadays spelled Glamis). The new lines opened for goods in 1837 and passengers in 1838, but neither were successful in generating new traffic or income. In 1841, the D&NR took a lease on the Newtyle & Couper Angus line but was unable to pay the rent.

Due to the poor financial state of the D&NR, the company at first looked into leasing the operation of the line or the line entirely to another company with a lease to the Dundee & Perth Railway coming into effect in July 1846 for £1,400 per annum for a period of 999 years. The D&PR immediately set about making improvements: the line was to be doubled; the Law tunnel was to be opened out and the Balbeuchly Incline was to be bypassed and many of the curves eased. The line was also regauged to British standard gauge, the work being completed in 1849. Unusually, the three Scottish-built locomotives were converted to standard gauge and continued to work on the line, but the more modern *John Bull* was sold. *Earl of Airlie* and *Lord Wharncliffe* would outlast the D&NR by many years and were reportedly still in operation in 1854. The former was taken out of service and used as a pumping engine at Errol railway station, while the latter was used at the railway works in Dundee, also as a pump. During the early 1860s, Alexander Allen, the locomotive superintendent of the Scottish Central Railway, recognised the historical importance of the *Earl of Airlie* and had it cosmetically restored and photographed. Tragically, it was not preserved which was a great loss for Scottish railway history. It was only in 1859 that an Act enabled the bypassing of the steep inclines: the Balbeuchy avoiding line came into use in 1860 and the Lochee deviation in 1861, but the Newtyle incline remained in use until 1868 when the work was carried out by the Caledonian Railway.

Garnkirk & Glasgow (1831)

The Garnkirk & Glasgow Railway was primarily formed to carry coal from the Monkland coalfield to Glasgow. It was laid to a gauge of 4 ft 6 in, using wrought-iron fish-belly rails on stone blocks. As it connected with the M&KR, they used the same gauge rather than the G&GR adopting 4 ft 8½ in. The gauge was altered to 'standard' when it was purchased by the Caledonian Railway, most of the work being undertaken during 1847. It was the first railway in Scotland to use 'modern' locomotives, both of which were supplied by Robert Stephenson & Co. of Newcastle upon Tyne. The first, *St Rollox*, was a typical member of the 2-2-0 Planet class but was somewhat smaller than usual, with smaller cylinders and a smaller boiler. The second locomotive was an 0-4-0 Samson type named *George Stephenson*. The G&G, therefore, marks the end of the 'early' railways period of Scotland and the beginning of the 'early mainline' period, one which sadly saw the loss of a distinctive Scottish railway identity as the railway network grew and became part of a British network.

The G&GR was envisaged as a coal railway serving Glasgow, but most of its mineral traffic would originate not at coal and fireclay pits around Garnkirk, but rather from the M&KR which the G&GR joined at Bedlay near Muirhead. An Act of Parliament of 26 May 1826 authorised construction of the line with a capital of £28,497 17*s*. 4*d*. Thomas Grainger and John Miller (above) were appointed as engineers and the first sod was

A contemporary depiction of the *George Stephenson,* built for the Garnkirk & Glasgow Railway by Robert Stephenson & Co. Although not the first locomotive to run in Scotland, it was the first modern locomotive. (Anthony Dawson)

ceremonially cut on 28 August 1827. Construction was delayed due to bad weather and lack of finances. A second Act had to be obtained in 1830 to enable the company to raise an additional £21,150. The first revenue traffic was carried in March 1831, when coal was sent eastwards from Gartcloss Colliery for onward travel via the M&KR. During May 1831 horse-drawn coal trains from Monklands to Glasgow started operating. The formal

The opening day of the G&GR, as depicted by David Octavius Hill, showing the trains hauled by the *George Stephenson* (Samson type) and *St Rollox* (Planet type) crossing each other. (Anthony Dawson)

opening of the line to the public would have to wait until the first locomotives arrived from England.

St Rollox was despatched from Newcastle upon Tyne on 20 May 1831, arriving in Glasgow in July 1831. She underwent a 'trial trip' 'amid the cheering of a considerable concourse of spectators':

> Having had the pleasure of witnessing the starting of a steamer, and experience the agreeable sensations produced by a whirl through the air at the rate upwards of twenty miles an hour, we must say that the utility as well as safety of such a mode of conveyance has been clearly demonstrated... The carriage for the passengers, the 'Isabella' is a handsomely constructed machine, divided into three nicely cushioned compartments, fit to accommodate eight persons each... The 'St Rollox' is only meant to propel passengers.
>
> *Star* (London), 13 July 1831

In fact, this steam-powered passenger service was only marginally predated by a horse-hauled service which began on 1 June 1831. The opening train of the G&GR on 27 September 1831 was headed by *St Rollox*, departing from the St Rollox Depot. The train consisted of one open carriage carrying the Airdrie Instrumental Band, three more open carriages and two enclosed carriages, the 'Royal William' and 'Royal Adelaide', with some 200 passengers on board including the Lord Provost, magistrates and members of the council of the City of Glasgow. The train departed Glasgow at 12.30 p.m. and, upon reaching the halfway point, was passed by a train headed by the *George Stephenson* running in the opposite direction (from Gartsherrie) with a train of thirty-two waggons, three of which were 'filled with another instrumental band and passengers', the other twenty-nine waggons being loaded with coal. The two engines met 'with the most deafening cheering' and went on to arrive at each terminus at 1.30 p.m. Preparations were then made for the locomotives to take their trains back to their respecting starting points at about 2.30 p.m. The *George Stephenson* took a load of eighteen waggons carrying many of the men who had built the railway, but about halfway an additional sixteen waggons were coupled to the front of the engine (!) and with this load, estimated at upwards of 100 tons, carried on her way, attaining a speed of about 18 mph. The *St Rollox* made her return trip with a train of eight carriages and arrived 'at the Depot about three o'clock'. The *George Stephenson* made a third trip around 6.00 p.m., this time with thirty-one coal waggons, twenty-eight loaded with coal and with 'workmen and colliers clinging around to form four or six on each waggon'. The other three were loaded with passengers. The total load was estimated to be 118 tons.

The Glasgow terminus of the G&GR was in the Townhead district, to the north-east of the city centre. It was built at what was then part of Keppochhill Road and which is now called Glebe Street. The 'passenger shed' was located on the east side of Glebe Street and the 'carriage shed' on the opposite side. The engine shed was further to the east. By 1839 there was a 'small booking-office and passenger-hall' for the accommodation of passengers. At Gartsherrie there was an inn which also acted as the station house where passengers could purchase tickets and wait for a train. The Gartsherrie Inn opened in summer 1832, having been built by the G&GR. The first landlord was 'Mr Wilson, late of the Caledonian Inn,

A splendid depiction by D. O. Hill of the two opening day trains meeting at St Rollox, looking south-east. (Anthony Dawson)

Hill's depiction of the Germiston embankment, looking west. (Anthony Dawson)

The Glasgow depot of the G&GR, as drawn by Hill on the opening day. *St Rollox* is arriving with a coal train and the yard is filled with coal wagons, emphasising the G&GR's primary role as a coal carrier. (Anthony Dawson)

Glasgow under whose active and judicious management every convenience is afforded'. As the 'intermediate traffic is but small', none of the two or three other 'stopping places' on the line were provided with passenger accommodation.

St Rollox was sold in 1837, possibly because even by that date it was too small for the work required, to the Paisley & Renfrew Railway for £350 and worked there until scrapping in 1848. According to Francis Whishaw, who visited the line in 1839, the G&GR possessed six locomotives and by this date *St Rollox* had been taken out of use; George Stephenson, however, was still suggesting that *St Rollox* was too small for the traffic. Two further Samson-type locomotives had been built locally for the G&G: the *Glasgow*, built by Messrs Johnston & Macnab of Glasgow, which first ran on 1 March 1832, and the *Garnkirk*, built by Murdoch, Aitken & Co. of Hill Street Foundry, Glasgow, in 1832. Two other locomotives were supplied by Murdoch, Aitken & Co.: the *Gartgill* of 1833, a heavy-weight 0-6-0, and the *Jenny* of 1835, a Planet type. The sixth was the 0-4-0 *Frew*, built by the St Rollox Foundry Company.

The G&GR had not originally been intended to be a passenger line, but by 1839 it had a stock of eighteen closed and open passenger carriages, which were described as being 'by far the most unsightly and uncomfortable we have ever met on any passenger-railway in the United Kingdom'.

An extension to Coatbridge – which was not welcomed by the M&KR! – had been in the air since 1837 but only got off the ground in 1843. The need for the branch arose because

The Gartsherrie Inn was opened by the G&GR in 1832 for the sale of refreshments (including alcohol) and tickets and to provide waiting accommodation. (East Dunbartonshire Archives)

This image of a train on the Liverpool & Manchester Railway gives a good impression of what travel was like on the G&GR. In just over a century, Scotland's railways were transformed from the wooden Tranent–Cockenzie Waggonway to mainline railways operated by locomotives and were the start of a national network. (Anthony Dawson)

the M&KR refused to allow locomotives, or at least G&GR locomotives, on its line. This led to G&GR deciding to build its own independent line paralleling, and bypassing, the M&KR, which would connect with the Wishaw & Coltness Railway which sent a lot of its coal traffic over the M&KR. To build the extension, the G&GR had to seek parliamentary authority, and to regularise its new position, it changed its name to the Glasgow, Garnkirk and Coatbridge Railway on 19 July 1844. The new company did not last long, however, as both it and the M&KR were absorbed by the Caledonian Railway in August 1846.

Summary

Whilst the railway came somewhat late to Scotland in 1722, as shown in earlier chapters, there was a flourishing cross-border transfer of technology. The first proposal for a locomotive in Scotland came only twelve months after their successful commercial introduction at the Middleton Railway in Leeds, although this did not result in the construction of an actual locomotive. The first locomotive in Scotland, an English import, steamed in 1816 only two years after George Stephenson's faltering efforts at Killingworth Colliery in summer 1814. It would, however, be another fifteen years until a locomotive was built in Scotland for the Monkland & Kirkintilloch Railway, albeit to a modified Stephenson design. This kick-started Scotland's locomotive-building industry, culminating in the mighty North British Locomotive Company of 1903, which was the largest locomotive-building company in Europe and the British Empire.

Chapter 5

What to See and Places to Go

For the industrial heritage and early railway tourist, there are several offerings in Scotland which afford a range of experiences. From museums to surviving landscape features, there really is a lot out there to see and while a Beamish-scale attraction has not yet come to fruition, the trail of worthwhile sites is worth taking the time to explore.

The authors advise that whilst 'the right to roam' is a generally accepted principle in Scotland, it is always advisable to seek permission where sensible.

Publicly Accessible Field Locations

1722 Tranent–Cockenzie Waggonway

Most of the route of Scotland's earliest railway can be walked or cycled, either taking the form of roadside footpath or cross-country bridleway. The whole route is marked with blue and brown waymarkers.

The most recognisable part of the route is where it crosses the fields where the Battle of Prestonpans was fought in 1745. This section is defined by two walls running either side of a straight routeway which takes the line of both the original wooden, and subsequent iron, waggonways. This section of the route was built up during the nineteenth-century upgrades to the line and the raised embankment covers the in situ remains of the original wooden railway beneath.

At the southern end of the route, Tranent Heugh is a surviving 'coal heugh' where coal was hewn from the surface from a natural gully. The waggonway ran all the way up this gully to an eighteenth-century coal pit at the top.

At the northern end, Cockenzie Harbour sports stone sleepers embedded in the quayside and is a fabulously untouched piece of nineteenth-century industrial heritage. A short stretch of replica wooden waggonway is located on the coast, just to the east of the harbour pier.

Several stone sleeper blocks can be found around the area of Cockenzie, notably where School Lane meets New Street. Here, the gable end of the first house on New Street has many sleepers built into the upper section and chimney area. Also, at West Harbour Road, there are sleepers topping the wall adjacent to James Dickson's Fish Shop, and further

The 1722 Waggonway Heritage Centre has the most extensive collection of material relating to waggonways in Scotland. (Ed Bethune)

down towards the harbour a double set block with two pairs of holes can be found in the retaining wall near the Scottish Water building.

Edinburgh & Dalkeith Railway

Within the City of Edinburgh, the most obvious and easily accessible location of interest is that of a section of the Edinburgh & Dalkeith Railway, also known as 'The Innocent Railway'.

At Holyrood Park, a cycle track which follows the route is accessible from the main park road when entering the low road to Duddingston from the park entrance near the Royal Commonwealth Pool. Upon descending to the cycle track here, walkers and cyclists can either explore Scotland's first tunnel (on a public railway) to the north-west or follow the route south-east towards Duddingston. The route descends steadily to an intersection with Duddingston Road West, where interpretation information is available. From here, the cycle path continues to Niddrie, Bingam and Brunstane.

Also of note, and worth a visit, is the National Transport Trust 'Red Wheel' plaque which has been erected at the site of the former terminus of the line at St Leaonard's Station & Coal Depot. This is now the home of the Holyrood Distillery, accessed by Hermit's Croft or St Leonard's Lane.

The 'Innocent Railway' tunnel in Edinburgh, easily accessible from Holyrood Park. (Irid Escent – Creative Commons)

Fordell Railway

Much of the route of this colliery railway can still be found, if you know where to look.

Dalgety Bay station is a great starting point. From here it is possible to travel south to the remains of St David's Harbour, the southern terminus of the line, although this area is heavily developed and there is not a great deal to see along the way. Some stone sleeper blocks can still be found at the harbour – look for rebated settings with a pair of holes for the chair bolts.

To the north, there is much more opportunity for exploration. From the station, take the footpath to the northern side of the railway, and follow the footpath on a slightly circuitous route to link up with the large embankment to the east. It is a large landscape feature here, and easy to find. From here, the route can be explored northwards, and whilst a few slight diversions may be necessary, much of this line can be walked with ease through the picturesque farm and estate landscape.

Along the way, a particular highlight is the bridge/tunnel which carried the estate road over the railway en route to the now-demolished Fordell House.

Further north, the path gets lost on account of the Muirdean opencast mine. While the route is difficult to trace, there are detours available via local paths. This one really is about exploration and discovery.

The tunnel/bridge at Fordell House, under which the railway ran. (Bill Roberton)

Brora Mine & Waggonway, Sutherland

The landscape around Brora is complicated and challenging to navigate on account of the terrain and restrictive land boundaries, but it is worth a mention here because there are ways to explore. Local heritage groups can be contacted the via the Brora Heritage Centre and local guides show interested parties some of the key sites relating to the waggonways, coal pits and salt pans which were once at the forefront of a thriving industrial complex.

Museums and Heritage Centres

The 1722 Waggonway Heritage Centre and Walking Route

West Harbour Road, Cockenzie, EH32 0HX
www.1722waggonway.co.uk

Formed in 2018, the 1722 Waggonway Project has built a collection of artefacts relating to the waggonway, including sleepers, chairs and rail fragments from the nineteenth-century era of Scotland's first railway. The exhibition also includes a wide range of maps, plans and models which help visitors to interpret and make sense of the landscape around them. The outside of the museum sports a National Transport Trust 'Red Wheel' plaque, signifying the importance of this as a key transport heritage location.

Also worth a look are Mr Cadell's Office and William Dickson's Workshop, where you can step back in time for a moment in the recreated surroundings of the past. The knowledgeable staff will also be happy to arrange a personal tour of the local points of interest, including seeing remnants of the waggonway salt pans at Cockenzie Harbour. Entry is free.

A replica one-third-scale salt pan is also located nearby at Cockenzie House & Gardens, and is operated regularly by museum staff.

From the Waggonway Heritage Centre, walkers and cyclists can explore the waggonway route itself to the north, where the modern-day bridleway follows the original route all the way up the hill to Tranent, taking in the associated history of the battlefield where Bonnie Prince Charlie famously defeated the Hanoverians near Prestonpans in 1745.

The 2½-mile route is a mixture of paved paths and hardcore tracks and is waymarked by blue footpath signage and brown heritage signs.

Prestongrange Museum

Morrisons Haven, Prestonpans EH32 9RX
https://www.eastlothian.gov.uk/info/210593/museums/11878/museums_in_east_lothian/4

A 2-mile walk to the west along the John Muir Way coastal path from Cockenzie takes you to Prestongrange Museum, an open-air industrial heritage museum operated by East Lothian Council on the site of the former Prestongrange Colliery, which was also home to potteries, glassworks, brickworks and the harbour of Morison's Haven.

Visitors can wander freely in the network of paths around the site, where a Cornish beam engine, pit-head winding gear and a Hoffman brick kiln are all spectacular features. Another highlight is the newly built engine shed, which houses rolling stock from the twentieth-century colliery operations of the site.

Entry is free and the visitor centre has a range of exhibits telling the history of the site; audio tours are available to help guide visitors around the museum and parkland.

Museum of Scottish Railways

Bo'Ness station, Union Street, Bo'Ness, EH51 9AQ
www.museumofscottishrailways.org.uk

Located to the west of Edinburgh, Scotland's largest railway museum has a large collection of artefacts, including rolling stock, locomotives and railway infrastructure. Visitors to the museum can enjoy the displays which tell the story of Scotland's railways and access the

Prestongrange Open Air Industrial Heritage Museum has a Cornish beam engine, Hoffman kiln and many items of rolling stock. (Ed Bethune)

extensive educational resources both on site and online. Also on the site is the Bo'Ness and Kinneil Railway, which runs steam services throughout the year.

Summerlee Museum of Scottish Industrial Life

Heritage Way, Coatbridge, ML5 1QD
www.culturenl.co.uk/museums/visiting-us/summerlee/

The Museum of Scottish Industrial Life is located at the site of the former Summerlee Iron Works and Hydrocon Crane Factory. It is a heritage hub which celebrates the lives of the working people who lived and worked around the engineering, mining, steelworking, weaving and farming industries through the nineteenth and twentieth centuries. A particular highlight for visitors is an operational heritage tramway with passenger trams.

Additionally, the Miner's Row shows workers' homes of the period faithfully recreated and preserved.

The National Mining Museum Scotland

Lady Victoria Colliery, Newtongrange, Dalkeith, EH22 4QN
www.nationalminingmuseum.com

This museum showcases the national collection of artefacts relating to the history of mining in Scotland, amidst the stunning setting of Lady Victoria Colliery, one of the best-preserved Victorian coal mine sites in the country. Interactive exhibitions and guided tours help visitors understand the working lives of the mining communities which were the backbone of the industrial age in Scotland. As well as housing an extensive archive of reference material, the museum is also home to the national memorial for mining disasters in Scotland.

Museum of Lead Mining

Visitor Centre, Wanlockhead, ML12 6UT
www.leadminingmuseum.co.uk

Located in Wanlockhead, Scotland's highest village, this fascinating museum is a unique and authentic visitor destination, with mine tours available and period cottages from eighteenth to twentieth centuries offering a glimpse into the working and living conditions of lead miners and their families. Gold panning sessions are also available.

Brora Heritage Centre

Clynelish Road, Brora, KW9 6LS
www.broraheritage.com

Focusing on the history of the Brora Coal Mine, which had a 400-year lifespan and was home to various waggonway lines, and the salt industry of the area, this excellent museum and visitor centre has extensive exhibits from archaeological digs in the area, conducted by the Clyne Heritage Society. Also on site is a one-third-scale replica salt pan constructed by the 1722 Waggonway Project team as part of inter-heritage group collaboration focused on shared coal and salt history.

Final Thoughts

Scotland's early railways, particularly the wooden ones, have often been overlooked. When we think of railways, we think in terms of the more robust modern infrastructure characterised by the age of steam locomotives and the Victorian age of industry.

But the eighteenth-century wooden horse-drawn waggonways and the innovative, evolutionary designs which bridged the gap to the coming of the iron railway are hugely significant. From the 1722 Tranent–Cockenzie Waggonway onwards, eighteenth-century Scotland quickly harnessed the uses of railed transport in industry and rolled with it. The salt industry had a big part to play in catalysing the need for early railways; after all it was the largest industrial manufacturing process of the time and without it, would the need for the colliery waggonways have come about so soon? Around the country from 1722 onwards, just about every salt works brought in its fuel by rail once they got their act together. The symbiosis of salt, coal and waggonways cannot be underestimated. Furthermore, unlike in England, many of these railways although built primarily to serve the interests of colliery owners, provided facilities for townspeople and local industries including distilling, brick

An early wooden waggonway. (Illustrated by Alan Braby)

and tile making as well as glass making. The close relationship between coal, iron and the railways drove expansion of the Scottish iron industry at centres such as Carron and later around Glasgow, as well as Scotland's own locomotive-building industry.

And what have they left us? The early railways of Scotland sparked and facilitated the growth of the nation through the Industrial Revolution. As with railways across the British Isles and the globe, our society is built on their success. The legacy they have left is integral to the world we live in today. It is huge part of the story of the working people and their way of life. It is an unavoidable part of our history. So, places where we can learn about, celebrate and experience the heritage of these very early industrial lines are vital and must be supported. Many of the places to visit rely on volunteers, and support of these projects and institutions is essential to ensure that the research, fieldwork and heritage legacy is preserved for future generations. Visit, learn and enjoy.

Bibliography and Further Reading

The following books and journal articles have been referenced in the production of this book. Given its length and scope, we present them here as both bibliography and further reading. Some of them, however, are showing their age whilst others, such as Worling, contain errors especially regarding the Tranent–Cockenzie Waggonway.

Bethune, Ed, Gareth Jones, Alan Braby, Gary Donaldson and Aaron Allen, 'Cockenzie, 1722, and the Recovery of a Saltwork Community' in Christopher Whatley and Joanna Hambly (eds), *Salt. Scotland's Newest Oldest Industry* (Edinburgh: John Donald, 2023)

Dawson, Anthony, 'Rebuilding the Tranent-Cockenzie Waggonway: public experimental archaeology', *EXARC* (forthcoming)

Dendy Marshall, C. F., *A History of British Railways down to the year 1830* (Oxford: Oxford University Press, 1938)

Dott, George, *Early Scottish Colliery Wagonways* (Westminster: St Margaret's Technical Press Ltd, 1947)

Dott, George, 'Early Scottish colliery waggonways. Part 2', *Colliery Engineering* (June 1947), pp. 195–200

Ferguson, Niall, *The Dundee & Newtyle Railway* (Oxford: The Oakwood Press, 1995)

Lewis, Michael J. T., *Early Wooden Railways* (London: Routledge Kegan & Paul, 1970)

Martin, Don, *The Garnkirk & Glasgow Railway* (Glasgow: Strathkelvin District Libraries, 1981)

Martin, Don, *The Monkland & Kirkintilloch and Associated Railways* (Glasgow: Strathkelvin District Libraries, 1995)

Paxton, Roland, 'An Engineering Assessment of the Kilmarnock & Troon Railway (1807–1846)' in Andy Guy and Jim Rees (eds), *Early Railways* (London: Newcomen Society, 2001)

Robertson, C. J. A., *Origins of the Scottish Railway System 1722–1848* (Edinburgh: John Donald Publishers Ltd, 1983)

Whishaw, Francis, *The Railways of Great Britain and Ireland* (London: John Weale, 1842)

Worling, M. J., *Early Railways of the Lothians* (Midlothian District Libraries, 1991)

Acknowledgements

We'd like to thank those who helped us along the (waggon)way in making this book happen. Firstly, Alan Braby, not only for his archaeological insights, but also for his superb illustrations and models. The members and volunteers of the 1722 Waggonway Project, who continue to work tirelessly to uncover the past. Paul Jarman, John New and Bill Roberton for photographs, and Richard Garside and Dan Lohrenz as experimental archaeological subjects. We must also mention the many organisations and people which have been fabulous to deal with in providing material for use in this publication: Cockenzie House & Gardens, Jill Turnbull, Battle of Prestonpans (1745) Heritage Trust, National Library of Scotland, Brora Salt Pans Research Group, East Lothian Council Museums Service, North Lanarkshire Museums and East Dunbartonshire Archives.

And last, but by no means least, our long-suffering families for their never-ending patience.